THAILAND

past and present

G. MALPEZZI

BARNES & NOBLE

NEW YORK

1 Coconuts are served without their outer shell and ready to drink by a vendor as she slips through the floating market on her boat.

2-3 Inside the enclosure of Wat Phra Kheo, dozens of little yellow candles and incense sticks left by worshippers burn in bowls and racks provided for offerings.

4-5 For Buddhists, gold is a symbol of spiritual purity. However, in the glittering splendor of the Temple of the Emerald Buddha, or Wat Phra Keo,

in Bangkok, among the fanciful creatures of Hindu mythology, the monks' saffron-colored robes remind visitors that the greatest value in life is simplicity.

CONTENTS

Graphic design
Maria Cucchi

© 2004 White Star S.p.a.

This edition published by
Barnes & Noble Publishing, Inc.,
by arrangement
with White Star S.p.a.

2006 Barnes & Noble Books

M10987654321
isbn-13: 978-0-7607-8263-7
isbn-10: 0-7607-8263-6

Translation
Timothy Stroud
Amy Ezrin

Library of Congress
Cataloging-in-Publication
Data available

Color separation Fotomec, Turin
Printed in Indonesia

6-7 Seen from above, the city stretches as far as the eye can see along the banks of the Chao Phraya River. On the Thonburi side the main phrang of Wat Arun stands out, about 280 feet tall, sitting on multiple terraces and surrounded by smaller pavilions with pointed roofs and porcelain-tiled spires.

7 top left Against the background of granite mountains, which look like dragons fallen into an eternal sleep, slipping down until they drop off into the waters of a thousand little inlets, the typical landscape of rice paddies and forests of Thailand's southern regions extends over the level plains.

7 top right The true name of the oldest temple and monastery in Bangkok, Wat Po, is Wat Phra Chetupon, the temple of the Reclining Buddha. The statue, 148 feet long and 49 feet high, is made of gold-leafed plaster-covered bricks, and the soles of its feet are inlaid with the 108 well-wishing signs of Buddhism.

6 Humidity and the mark of time cannot diminish the purity of the lines of the stupas at Wat Phra Si Sanphet, in Ayuthaya, the ancient capital. Their bell shape sits on a several-tiered base and is surmounted by the harmika, a balustrade supporting a pinnacle.

Thailand is the "gateway to the East," where the opulence of India is lightened by the grace of Southeast Asia. It is a world of water, green rice paddies, and mountains that melt into the blue of the sky, as ancient as old sleeping dragons. In this world, purple orchids blossom everywhere, in the jungle and on the trees of the big cities, the temples have pointed roofs that seem covered in jewels, and the image of Buddha is slender and ascetic, yet wrapped in gold. These images of apparent fragility correspond to a country that has succumbed completely to the reality of modern times without losing any of its traditional values. Like other Asian peoples, the Thai have known how to live in society, they respect social hierarchies, and they follow the rules that govern civil co-existence. Forever smiling, they have a relaxed and serene way of doing things, and as they say in every situation, "*mai pen rai*," everything should be done calmly, it is not necessary to rush. Despite their attitude, they are neither compliant nor weak and have an extremely strong personality. For this reason, since time immemorial, any foreign cultural contributions have been revised to become Thai. Even if Western economic systems have been adopted, making Thailand one of the emerging "tigers" of Asia, it has not compromised the country's independence or individuality, just as in the past, it has avoided falling into the colonial trap yet still been able to take advantage of relations with the West thanks to skillful diplomacy. Though Bangkok is a highly modern metropolis, with head-spinning skyscrapers and a subway system that speeds by above ground like in a science-fiction film, the country has maintained intact its spiritual and traditional world.

Thailand is a country of water. There is the water of the rice paddies that look like mirrors laid out on the ground to reflect the sky and the outline of the pagodas. There is also the water of the canals, which insinuate themselves into people's lives by having the same role as roads, the only difference being that boats can float on them and one can jump into them to combat the heat. Traditional houses have their front door on the canal, the *khlong*, and not on the street, their porch extends over the water on stilts, and once upon a time, but perhaps still today in the countryside, merchants slipped from house to house selling fruit and rice, and in a big pan, cooked food to sell on their boats, a sort of water-borne take-out.

Once upon a time, by way of the canals, rice was exported to China, where it was paid for in precious goods for being so good and fragrant. Transportation took place on big wide boats and on barges, just like those that can still be seen slowly skimming by on the river's current, among the elegant little palaces and skyscrapers of Bangkok, through the traffic of the ferries carrying worshippers to Wat Arun, and slowly, without haste, slipping toward the shadow of the temples of Ayutthaya.

Thailand is a country of four aspects. The strip of land that stretches as far as the Malaysian Peninsula features the luxuriant tropical plantations reaching out toward a turquoise- and sapphire-colored sea. The coast climbs up toward the Gulf of Siam with a sequence of white beaches that curve to form tranquil bays, where only the rustle of the palm trees in the wind and the breaking of the waves break the silence. The hills descend toward the sea and seem to pulverize into thousands of islands, which hide the magical and silent world of the coral reefs. Many are completely deserted, and those who wish to live a Robinson Crusoe or Gauguin fantasy can make a reservation with the Forest Department. They will be assigned a place to stay in either a tent or a bungalow on an island that is not already occupied by other, however few, tourists. Alternatively, it is possible to rent a sailboat with a skipper and stop to swim to the beaches of marine parks, where it is not allowed to stay because the ecosystems must not be contaminated. Not even the sea's fury could alter the environmental and human situation on the country's west coast for long, where some of the islands best known to tourists are found. The tsunami that, at the end of 2004, wiped out the existence of hundreds of thousands of people in just a few hours will of course never be forgotten, but the Thai's determination to not let themselves be overwhelmed by the catastrophe has been so dogged, and so great the force of nature in dismissing old wounds, that the wave's passing has almost left no visible traces. Even the northeast has been preserved intact from an environmental point of view thanks to a wise economic policy based on agriculture and the construction of dams and irrigation canals instead of industrialization. Besides the traditional agricultural products, cattle-raising was introduced, to provide meat and dairy products, as well as viticulture, which has given rise to some excellent wines, never produced before. It is a pleasure to travel mile after mile through forests and across lands planted with rice, passing through villages where the people live a traditional lifestyle but with the amenities furnished by modern technology. These are the borderlands along the Mekong River, where the prehistoric inhabitants settled, and where Laotians, Cambodians, Chinese, and Vietnamese come to sell their crafts and goods at the big market of Mukdahan.

10 bottom Settled mostly in the mountainous areas of the provinces of Chiang Rai, Phayao, and Nan, the Yao speak a language in the Austro-Thai family. They cultivate rice in dry fields, practice polygamy, and have adopted the Chinese alphabet for sacred writings, oracles, and also contracts.

The north offers another aspect of Thailand. Beyond the central plains, flat and suited to rice and tropical fruit growing, the mountainous region of Chiang Mai begins, the ancient Lannathai, the kingdom of teak forests and elephants, and the border between Thailand and the vast regions of China. It is a zone of hills covered with vegetation and full of rivers that flow down to become big in the plains of the south, where the Karen, Yao, and Meo ethnic groups live in villages once dedicated to cultivating opium poppies. Here, spirits live alongside man, temples have enormous roofs and three-light façades, and houses bear the good-luck charm of buffalo horns on top. The climate is cooler than in the south, where monsoons make the weather even hotter

10 top Streams run down from the mountains of the north, transforming into waterfalls and continuing on towards the central valleys. The waters of a thousand little rivulets from the northern jungle then combine in the majestic rivers of Thailand, only to fragment again into the canals of the rice paddies and the cities.

10-11 In order to never forget the cold regions of China or distant Central Asia from where they originate, the Hmong (also known as the Meo) decorate their already flashy traditional clothing with snowflake patterns and triangles and silver coins hung on strings of little pearls.

11 As the river's waters wind through the tropical vegetation, they lose strength, until they flatten out like pools of mud. Here at Prou Chumphon, time seems to have come to a standstill in some remote era, crystallized in all its pristine beauty.

and more humid from April to October, and it is possible to hike along mountain trails through wild forests that are relatively smooth.

The Thai language is a tonal language, in the sense that the tone determines the meaning of the word. For example, the syllable *kao* can mean news, white, or rice according to the tone in which it is pronounced. Even though in the north, northeast, and south different dialects are spoken, the national language is that derived from the spoken language of Bangkok and the central regions. It is very similar to Laotian, but different from Burmese, Cambodian, and Malaysian. Although not structurally difficult since its verbs have no conjugation, it presents some difficulty of pronunciation for speakers of either Romance or Anglo-Saxon languages because of its unusual sounds. It is written in its own alphabet derived from the that of the languages of southern India, from left to right on horizontal lines, with the vowels indicated at times above and at times below the consonant, and without spaces between the words. No official transliteration into the Latin alphabet having been approved, its sounds are generally transcribed as an English-speaker would pronounce them, thus it is possible to find several different spellings for words, especially for geographical names. Is it Tailand or Thailand? Chiang Mai or Cheng Mai? The important thing is to be understood, and in the end, it is not so difficult when confronted with a Thai smile and the sweetness of their hello: *sawadee*!!

Laos

Myanmar (Burma)

Vietnam

Chiang Mai
Lamphun
Lampang
Nan
Mekong River
Nakhon Phanom
Bumibol Reservoir
Udon Thani
Si Satchanalai
Sukhothai
Phitsanulok
Mae Nam Yom
Mekong
Nakhon Sawan
Ubolratana Reservoir
Lam Pao Reservoir
Nakhon Ratchasima
Ubon Ratchathani
Mae Nam Mun
Khao Laem Reservoir
Si Nakharun Reservoir
Chao Phraya River
Ayutthaya
Surin
Kwai Noi
Kanchanaburi
Ratchaburi
Bangkok
Phetchaburi
Chon Buri
Pattaya
Cambodia
Hua Hin
Chantaburi
Trat

Andaman Sea

Bay of Bangkok

Ko Phangan
Ko Samui

Gulf of Thailand

Phang Nga
Nakhon Si Thammarat
Phuket
Ko Phi Phi
Phattalung
Ko Tarutao
Songkhla
Hat Yai

Gulf
of
Tonkin

13 top The dancers of Saraphi are distinguished by their grace and beauty.

13 bottom Phang Nga Bay is one of the best known in the country and well represents the lush landscape of the Thai seashore.

14-15 Rambutan, mangos, passion fruit, and rose apples are the *tropical delights offered by vendors at the floating market to their clients, as they slip from house to house down the canals. In Bangkok, a modern metropolis, the traditional floating market takes place discreetly at dawn, along the canals of the outskirts.*

16-17 The fertility of the land alone is not *enough to guarantee abundant harvests. For thousands of years, Thai farmers have learned to cultivate every last bit of their land, even the beaches, by regulating irrigation routines, keeping the fury of the monsoons in check, and protecting the crops from the harsh, burning sun.*

THE THOUSAND BATTLES OF THE KING

*T*he most ancient human settlement in Thailand dates back to about 5,600 years ago. Located in Ban Chiang in the northeast, recent excavations there have brought to light finds from a community dedicated to farming and livestock-raising, which worked metal using advanced techniques and produced attractive ceramics in a cream color with red spiral decorative drawings. However, legends speak of the descent of peoples from China, and in fact, in 2,500 B.C., some Proto-Malaysians appear to have settled in the Kanchanaburi region, west of Bangkok, while farmers from the Lungshan culture had imported sophisticated rice-cultivation methods into the Lopburi area. Between 1770 and 140 B.C., together with the Thai, groups of Mon and Khmer came south from the Yunnan.

The Thai peoples, who over 5,000 years ago had settled in northern Mongolia, migrated down toward the Yellow River and into Sichuan and organized themselves into city-states, but later, following nomad invasions, moved farther south until establishing themselves in Laos and Myanmar, along the Irrawaddy and Salween rivers, where they are known as Shan. The Thai who remained in China unified under the kingdom of Nan Chao, which, during the period of the Three Kingdoms (220-280 CE) conquered vast territories between Sichuan and Tibet. With the marriage of a Chinese princess to the king of Nan Chao, the state began to sinicize, until it became, for all intensive purposes, a Chinese province in 1253. These events induced the more independent groups to move toward the north of Thailand, whose descendants of Thai ethnicity still live in the Yunnan today.

18 From Gupta India, Hindu culture spread throughout Southeast Asia by way of sea trading. In Thailand, from the 6th until the 13th century, the Indianized Dvaravati kingdom grew, ruled mostly by Mon and Khmer, who were settled in the central plains. The cult of the gods Vishnu (portrayed in this 6th-century statue) and Shiva became predominant in the Angkor Empire.

19 top Thai Buddhist art strongly demonstrates the esthetic influence of the Gupta period. In this meditating Buddha, which dates back to the end of the 6th century, the fullness of form seen in the head is of Indian origin, whereas the trim simplicity of the lines of the body reflects characteristics of Thai sculpture already in use.

19 bottom The wheel is a symbol of Buddhism, which began to spread through Thailand in the third century B.C. thanks to monks invited by Emperor Ashoka. This version, in the National Museum of Bangkok, is decorated with floral motifs, symbols of illumination.

The Thai of Laos founded the kingdom of Sibsong Chetai, which in the 8th century CE, under the leadership of King Khun Borom and his son Khun Lo, expanded as far as Luang Prabang and Vientiane. To avoid wars of succession, the king's younger sons were given men with which to found their own fiefdoms.

At that time, Thailand was divided into small states, each with their own area of influence. Their main source of income came from agriculture using the "slash and burn" system: farmable land was obtained by burning tracts of forest, the ashes serving as fertilizer, and was then sown. With this system, however, the fields were rendered barren within a few years. It was therefore necessary to let them lie fallow for a while and seek new lands to cultivate. Demographic growth made it even more crucial to find new spaces and this instigated conflicts between the small states. During the course of the local wars, defensive and offensive alliances were established, and as one state prevailed over the others, feudal states were created composed of small independent kingdoms governed by local princes and united under the hegemony of the most powerful state. Thus, from time to time Lanna, Sukhothai, or Ayutthaya became the most influential kingdom in Thailand, thanks to the personalities of strong and aggressive leaders, who with their armies assured vast regions of peace and prosperity. The smaller realms were obligated by the hegemonic state to furnish the weapons and their own armies in the event of war. Of course, loyalties or aspirations of independence and expansion on the part of vassals created a situation of extreme political fluctuation.

In 1239, Mengrai, the founder of the Lannathai kingdom, was born to a descendant of the son of Khun Borom of the Thai of Laos, Chiang Saen. Mengrai was the first great political personality to be remembered in Thai history. Lannathai means "land of a million rice paddies" because in that region each citizen had to produce at least five *muen*, about 130 pounds, of rice. The local princes were perennially at war to guarantee themselves a work force or soldiers, and when they conquered a territory, they deported its inhabitants and left the land deserted. Mengrai managed to subjugate all the local feudal lords and united them under the hegemony of Lanna. Besides a skilled general, he was a wise administrator, who tried to develop the economy and the arts. It is said that he had artists come from Burma to teach the local craftsmen the smelting procedures for casting bronze statues.

Many legends flourish about him: one day tracking his elephant, which had escaped into the forest, he came to the shore of the Kok River, and he liked the place so much that he built the city of Chiang Rai, meaning "elephant footprint," upon it. It is said that he succeeded in conquering the cities of Khoen, Lawa, and Lampoon by cunning, infiltrating the enemy kingdoms with his advisors. These men, having gained the trust of the rulers and advising them to take steps unpopular with their subjects, managed to deliver the cities into the hands of Mengrai almost without striking a blow. In 1281, Mengrai occupied Lampoon, the city built in 645 by the Mon and at the time governed by Princess Chamadevi in the place of her husband who had become a monk. On the other hand, Lampang was conquered by a duel between Mengrai's son, Khun Kram, and the enemy prince. According to tradition, warriors of noble descent had to fight on the back of elephants.

20 *The sculpture of the kingdoms of the north expresses the asceticism and spirituality of Buddha through full and sensual forms. The 15th-century Lan Na bronze head shown in the photograph features a broad nose, a continuous eyebrow, distinctly engraved eyes, fleshy lips, and an abundant head of curly hair that frames the face in the shape of a heart.*

21 *This 15th-century statue of Buddha in meditation comes from Chiang Saen, an important city for the arts in the north. The hands are in the* maravijaya *position (mudra), and on top of its head, it wears the* ushnisha, *which symbolizes supernatural wisdom and, in the style of the central kingdoms, is represented by a flame shape.*

22-23 The temples are often decorated with wall paintings, which reproduce, along with subjects of a religious nature, lively scenes from daily life. This detail, in Wat Phra Singh in Chiang Mai, features dignitaries and country folk playing with buffaloes in the water, juxtaposed on spatial planes.

23 The elephant is the emblematic animal of Thailand. White elephants, a royal prerogative, lived in stalls within the palace. Richly dressed with sumptuous Lan-Na-style canopies, like the one shown in the photograph, they carried the king in parades or battle.

The foundation of Chiang Mai, the "new city," in 1296 was also determined by an odd event: Mengrai, while hunting, was following two deer when his dogs disappeared into the dense forest. Following them, he saw a white rat with her four little rats running toward a Bodhi tree. Because it appeared to him to be an auspicious sign, he began construction of the city that became the capital of the Lanna kingdom in 1345, though he always preferred to reside at Chiang Rai. At the time of Mengrai's death in 1317, the kingdom of Lanna stretched across the whole north, encompassing even Pegu, the Mon and Ava capitals, and the capital of Burma. It remained independent until 1556, when it fell under the Burmese control. The Lanna were proud and crafty warriors: as early as 1412, they succeeding in beating the terrible Chinese army with their cunning, digging traps that they covered with leaves and then leading the enemy to fall into them. During the reign of Tilokarat (1441-1485), they defeated the army of Ayutthaya with three spies that infiltrated the enemy camp. During the night, they untied the elephants after cutting off their tails, and the animals, mad with pain, wrought havoc. Another time, command of an expedition against an enemy city was entrusted to the mother of Tilokarat, Princess Mahadevi. The governor of the enemy city was also a woman, who led a fierce resistance. This "battle of ladies" was finally won by the energetic Mahadevi, who had a cannon forged on site, bombarded the enemy with cannonballs, and overcame the city.

The majority of the Thai territory in the south was occupied by the Mon to the west and the Khmer to the east. Sukhothai was part of the Mon kingdom of Dvaravati (Haripunchai), but in the 11th century came under the control of the Khmer, the founders of the empire at Angkor who required that their subject states pay annual tributes. Besides Mon and Khmer, the city was inhabited by Thai from Farng and Yunnan. During the reign of Suryavarman II (ca. 1113-1150), the annual tribute also included large quantities of water for the sacred lake of Angkor Thom, a humiliating and exhausting obligation considering that the containers were made of heavy terracotta. Prince Thai Khun Bangklangtao Khun Sri Indradit or Phra Ruang came up with the idea of bamboo containers made water-resistant with resin. After a few years, the clever prince rebelled against the powers at Angkor and became king of Sukhothai in 1239. Rama Kamhaeng, the king's third son, reigned from 1275 until 1317 and extended the realm's domain as far as Annam, Pegu, and the Malaysian Peninsula. In fact, Chinese sources claim that his political influence stretched as far as Sumatra and that he dared to attack even Angkor. What is certain is that with a series of military campaigns, he managed to end Khmer power in Thailand.

The nucleus of the kingdom, Muang Sukhothai, was formed by a network of villages and small settlements that were called by the name of the walled city, thus Sukhothai did not physically occupy its subject territories but through its political

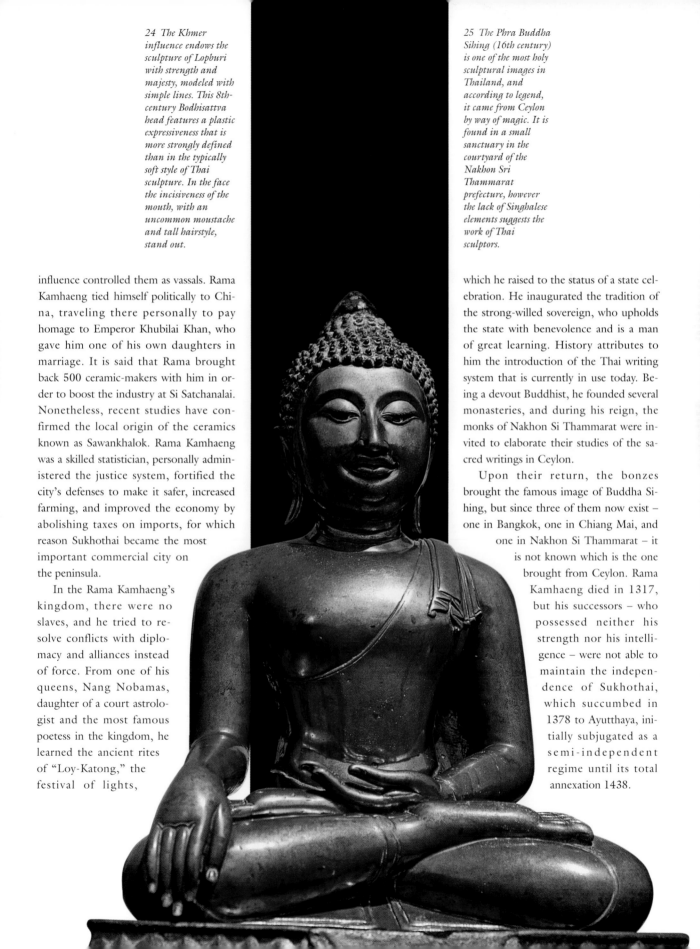

influence controlled them as vassals. Rama Kamhaeng tied himself politically to China, traveling there personally to pay homage to Emperor Khubilai Khan, who gave him one of his own daughters in marriage. It is said that Rama brought back 500 ceramic-makers with him in order to boost the industry at Si Satchanalai. Nonetheless, recent studies have confirmed the local origin of the ceramics known as Sawankhalok. Rama Kamhaeng was a skilled statistician, personally administered the justice system, fortified the city's defenses to make it safer, increased farming, and improved the economy by abolishing taxes on imports, for which reason Sukhothai became the most important commercial city on the peninsula.

In the Rama Kamhaeng's kingdom, there were no slaves, and he tried to resolve conflicts with diplomacy and alliances instead of force. From one of his queens, Nang Nobamas, daughter of a court astrologist and the most famous poetess in the kingdom, he learned the ancient rites of "Loy-Katong," the festival of lights, which he raised to the status of a state celebration. He inaugurated the tradition of the strong-willed sovereign, who upholds the state with benevolence and is a man of great learning. History attributes to him the introduction of the Thai writing system that is currently in use today. Being a devout Buddhist, he founded several monasteries, and during his reign, the monks of Nakhon Si Thammarat were invited to elaborate their studies of the sacred writings in Ceylon.

Upon their return, the bonzes brought the famous image of Buddha Sihing, but since three of them now exist – one in Bangkok, one in Chiang Mai, and one in Nakhon Si Thammarat – it is not known which is the one brought from Ceylon. Rama Kamhaeng died in 1317, but his successors – who possessed neither his strength nor his intelligence – were not able to maintain the independence of Sukhothai, which succumbed in 1378 to Ayutthaya, initially subjugated as a semi-independent regime until its total annexation 1438.

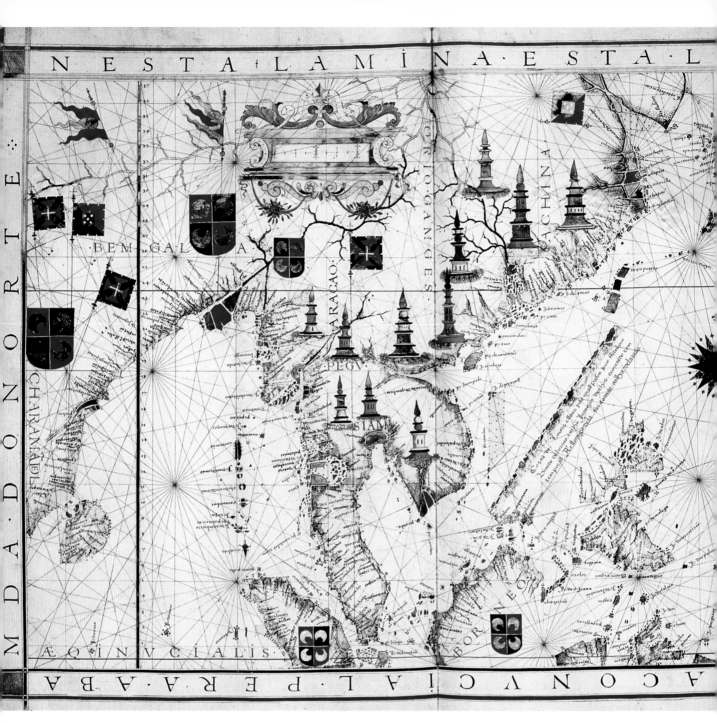

After fleeing the city set aflame by Shan conquerors, a prince and the survivors of Farng settled near Kampaengpet, and then at Nakhon Pathom. One of his descendants, who was married to the daughter of the king of Uthong, was forced to move the capital to Ayutthaya, at the time under Sukhothai control, in the wake of a cholera epidemic. He became the city's king in 1350, taking the name of Rama Thibodi. The kingdom of Ayutthaya, which covered North Laos, Pegu, the states of Shan and Martaban in Burma, the Malaysian Peninsula as far as Johore, and Cambodia at the time of its greatest expansion, was the most powerful Thai state until 1767. Its geographical position, impregnable but connected to the sea by a river, made it especially suitable for foreign trade, allowing it to become such a great power in the region. It exchanged a series of ambassadors with foreign countries, which from 1608 on were sent as far as the European courts to stipulate commercial treaties, giving the king monopolistic rights over imports and exports. His merchant fleets traded in an area ranging from Persia to Japan. From the Portuguese, the first foreigners allowed to settle in the city, Ayutthaya imported the firearms used to create a modern army commanded by Japanese military officers.

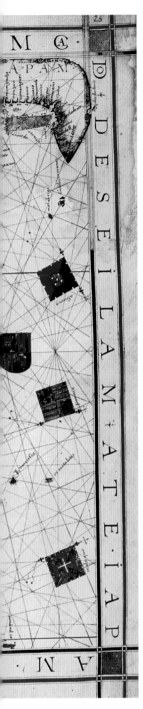

The French worked to strengthen the fortifications at Mergui and Bangkok, and their missionaries founded schools and a cathedral. The Dutch and British had each established mercantile depots by 1610. The king had men of diverse nationalities at his service; Phaulkon, a Greek who came to Ayutthaya in 1680 with the East India Company, even became prime minister to King Narai.

Much is known about Ayutthaya thanks to the accounts of Europeans who visited it. In 1567, it was bigger and had a greater population that both Paris and London; foreigners from 40 different countries resided there. It was a pretty and lively city, with paved streets shaded by trees and a complex network of canals crossed by wood or brick bridges. The urban center extended beyond its walls, into the boat-house villages, the Dutch mercan-

tile depots, and the colonies of the Japanese, Malaysians, Mon from Pegu, half-blood Portuguese, and the Dominican and Jesuit missions. Inside the walls, beautiful houses were inhabited by British, French, Dutch, Chinese, Indian, and Arab merchants, whereas the main street, which led to the palace, was crowded with shops and artisan workshops. Ships could dock in either the river harbor or in the canals within the city. The royal palace accommodated officers and government officials, around 100 royal elephants (some of which were white), and, in its inner courtyard, the pavilions of the king and the royal family, topped by golden spires. The king, one of the richest monarchs in the Orient, lived in absolute luxury, to the extent that his throne, according to the accounts of European travelers, was made of solid gold inlaid with precious stones.

27 Jesuit missionaries introduced the principles of modern science into the kingdom of Siam. The photo shows the fathers using a telescope to observe a solar eclipse in 1688. The king, at a window of the palace, witnesses the experiment.

26-27
The Portuguese were the first to draw maps of routes to countries producing exotic goods. They safeguarded their charts because they made it possible to maintain a monopoly over the trade routes. This map was drafted by Ferdinando Vaz-Dourado in 1573.

28 Paintings from Bangkok's greatest period embellish the walls of temples and palaces. This 18th-century wall painting portrays Buddha's descent from heaven. The figure of the Enlightened One descending a triple staircase and the flying Bodhisattvas, encircled by a bright-red aura, give the scene a fanciful lightness.

29 Upholding the Sukhothai tradition of simple lines and expressive intensity, over time the sculpture of Ayutthaya started to embellish figures with crowns and jewels. This head of Buddha (Ayutthaya style, 14th-century), though it maintains simplicity of form, features an accentuated expression of mysterious meditative serenity with a double line along the eyelids and lips.

The provinces were administered by governors upon whom was bestowed the power of the crown, who were required to supply armies in the event of war. On the other hand, the vassal states of Luang Prabang, Chiang Mai, Cambodia, and the Malaysian states were required to supply not only soldiers but to also pay tributes and visit the court, where their crown princes were educated.

The only rival of Ayutthaya was the Burmese state, which in 1564, after two centuries of fighting, besieged the Thai kingdom six times, managing to destroy it completely in 1767. In 1531, the Burmese King Tabinshweti, who had united parts of the Shan and Mon states under the control of Ava, politically controlled Chiang Mai and aimed to rule Vientiane and Ayutthaya. In 1548, Tabinshweti opened battle and would have killed King Maha Chakrapat of Ayutthaya, who having lost his balance had fallen from his elephant, had Queen Suriyothai not intervened to save her husband, dying, however, in the process. The Thai and their al-

lied forces forced the Burmese to retreat, but in pursuing them, the royal princes fell in an ambush and were taken prisoner by the enemy. To pay their ransom, the Thai King Maha Chakrapat handed over two of his white elephants, said to bring good luck, to Tabinshweti, who withdrew to Pegu.

Some time later, the Burmese king asked for additional white elephants. Upon refusal of the request – consent to which would have been considered an act of submission – he invaded Thai territory again. He first took control of all the northern cities, then occupied Pitsanuloke, and finally attacked Ayutthaya, which was forced to surrender. King Maha Chakrapat, along with his dignitaries and the actors of the court theater, was deported to Pegu, where he retired to a monastery.

In this way, the Thai ruling and intellectual classes were rendered harmless. A Burmese prince was named governor of the city while the army occupied the kingdom of Lanchang (Vientiane).

The resistance mounted by the citizens of Lanchang and Ayutthaya provoked violent reprisals by the Burmese, who sacked the Thai capital in 1569. The Thai prince Naresuen, son of the governor of Pitsanuloke, who was educated in Pegu while he was held hostage there, joined forces with the Mon, who had long suffered under Burmese oppression, and attacked Pegu, liberating the deported Thais, conquering the north, and laying siege to Ayutthaya. Naresuen was a great leader who knew who to make his soldiers proud to find for a just cause, and after having defeated the commanding prince of the Burmese army in a duel, ascended the throne of Ayutthaya in 1590. His victory was so absolute that all attacks from the west stopped until the mid-1700s. As for the east, in 1594, Naresuen reestablished control over the Cambodian vassals that had taken advantage of the situation to gain independence. Upon his death in 1605, the kingdom had secure borders and was once again powerful.

In 1656, the reign of Narai, Ayutthaya's greatest king, began, thus initiating a glorious period unfortunately also characterized by struggles to maintain the Thai territory intact. In Chiang Mai, Narai fell in love with a beautiful princess, with whom he had an illegitimate son, Luang Sorasak, who the king had one of his generals, Petraja, adopt. Narai was very fond of his natural son, and as he lay dying and without any direct heirs, plotted to place on the throne Luang Sorasak's adoptive father, Petraja, who married both Narai's sister and daughter to legitimize his position. The government of Petraja and the cruel Luang Sorasak, known as the Tiger King, and their successors further weakened the kingdom, to the extent that in 1760, the Burmese again attacked Ayutthaya. The final attack took place in 1764, when they seized the capital from the north, southwest, and by sea at Bangsai. Under siege, Ayutthaya fell on April 8, 1767. The Burmese, after sacking it, destroyed its temples, killed or deported its people, among whom were the survivors of the royal family, and set the city aflame. The booty taken, including firearms, gold, jewels, precious fabrics, and works of art, was enormous. Nonetheless, many of the city's riches were hidden by its citizens during the attack, and were only discovered many years later. The destruction was systematic and struck the city and its ruling class not only in a physical sense but also on a cultural level. In addition to the deportation of its artists, goldsmiths, weavers, magicians, astrologers, doctors and veterinarians, cooks, and musicians and dancers, the Buddhist canons and treatises on astrology and medicine were either destroyed or lost. When the Burmese withdrew in June 1767, nothing was left but a pile of ruins being picked over by

hungry stragglers. Apparently, the Thai were stronger that their enemies believed. Taksin, previously the governor of Tak, gathered together the remnants of the army and besieged the capital at Dhonburi, farther south on the banks of the Chao Phraya River. He was crowned king on December 28, 1768 and energetically dedicated himself its reconstruction. He began with the territory, taking back Pitsanuloke to the north and the territories to the east, going as far as Siem Reap and Battambang in order to ensure an alliance with the Cambodians against the expansionistic aims of the Annamese Empire, which could have joined forces with the Burmese to divide up the Thai territory. Beginning in 1776, he moved south as far as Nakhon Si Thammarat, completing the reconquest of the north from Chiang Mai to Laos. The Emerald Buddha, stolen in 1550, was brought back to Bangkok, where it can be seen today. At the same time, Taksin concentrated on reorganizing the legal system and rewriting the Buddhist canons. Cultured, intelligent, and an excellent writer, he revitalized the arts, literature, and the theater, seeking to reconstruct all that had been lost. He devoted himself to meditation, but it was not enough to save him from the stress of war and governing. During the 1779 military campaign in Cambodia, Taksin's mind began to waver, and a series of unpopular acts, most likely suggested by a power-seeking faction, set off a revolt, leading the king to retire to a monastery. He died on April 7, 1782, the same day he was born.

Navkeurige Beschryvinge Van het KONINGRYCK SIAM door de Heer IEREMIAS VAN VLIET

30 top The appearance of the ambassador of Siam intrigued French citizens of the 1680s and stirred artists' imaginations. In a 1686 print, Johann Hainzelmann reproduced the exotic face, opulent silk clothing, and curious cone-shaped, gold-decorated hat of Tan Oc-Cun Sri Saranacha Tritud.

30 bottom Sea commerce along the spice routes aroused great interest in 17th-century Europe in the Orient. Tales of period voyages now provide a valuable source of historical information. The frontispiece of this 1692 Dutch book provides images of the pagodas, pointed-roof temples, and elephants of Siam.

31 Siam was respected by the European superpowers as a sovereign state thanks to the skilled foreign policy of King Narai. Several diplomatic missions were invited to France, England, Portugal, and Holland. In 1686, the Siamese ambassador, shown in this print in a meeting with King Louis XIV, was welcomed with great ceremony to the court of Versailles.

LA SOLENNELLE AMBASSADE DU ROY DE SIAM AU ROY, POUR L'ESTABLISSEME
DU COMMERCE AVEC CES PEUPLES D'ORIENT, LES CEREMONIES DE LA LETTRE ET DES AUDIENCES.

AUDIENCE DU ROY DONNEE AUX AMBASSADEURS DU ROY DE SIAM

ALLIANCE DE LA FRANCE AVEC LE ROY DE SIAM

ALMANACH POUR L'ANNÉE M.DC.LXXXVII.

A PARIS, chez JEAN BAPTISTE NOLIN, ruë S. Jacques à l'enseigne de la Place des Victoires.

He was succeeded by his inseparable friend, and at the time prime minister, Tong Duang Chao Phraya Chakri, who took the name of Rama I. Born in 1737 in Ayutthaya, Rama I came from a noble family of Mon origin, to whose members the king had entrusted delicate and important government offices. His great-grandfather Kosaparn had been King Narai's ambassador to the French court and then prime minister. His father had been nominated Chao Phya Chakri, indicating a noble of Pitsanuloke's first class. He was educated at the temple of Maha Talai and sent to court

as a page, where he formed a close friendship with Taksin, with whom he went on to fight against the Burmese and reconquer of Thai territory. One of the first acts of his reign was to institute a policy of religious tolerance and friendly relations with the West. This conduct was very wise in that it avoided any meddling in state affairs by foreigners, who essentially only wanted to trade and get rich. The new king's policy thus guaranteed Thai independence during the era of colonial expansion. He moved the royal palace, the seat of the government, to a more strategic position in

Bangkok. However, the situation remained difficult: although Laos and Cambodia were tied to the Thai kingdom, Vietnamese power threatened the integrity of the eastern territory, and the Burmese were not about to give up their periodic attacks – attacks that occupied Thai defenses to the north, center, and the south on the sea, leaving the east vulnerable, easy prey for the Vietnamese. Although the hegemony of the Malaysian sultans was consolidated, from 1802 on a new fact contributed to rendering the situation more complicated. Now in control of Burma, the British, in supporting

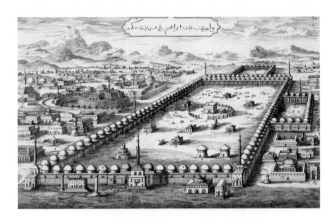

32-33 The Ratanakosin style is well exemplified by this painting, which portrays the division of the relics of Buddha after cremation.

33 top Bangkok in the 18th century: the Royal Palace looks enormous in this print from a 1721 book on architecture by Johann A. Delsenbach.

33 bottom In the paintings of the ubosot in Wat Ko Kaeo Suttharam at Petchaburi, depth is suggested by subdivision into alternating triangular forms.

the sultan of Kedah's aspirations of independence, were trying to infiltrate Thailand. The government at Bangkok succeeded in resolving the potential conflict through diplomacy, handing over Penang Island and a land grant on the mainland, at an annual rent of 6,000 Spanish dollars, to the British of the East India Company in 1791.

The kingdom gained a new law code, known as the "law of the three seals." To reconstruct the sacred writings of the Tripitaka Buddhist canon, a commission of 218 scholars to gathered at Wat Mahatat. After five months of work, they presented the

new edition to the library of Wat Phra Keo. Wat Mahatat remained the main center for Buddhist studies. In 1796, some French missionaries introduced the printing press into Thailand and, by transliterating the Thai alphabet into Latin letters, opened the first printing works in Bangkok.

Rama I died in 1809 and Lert-Lah Rama II, his son, became the first monarch to govern in times of peace, which he was able to maintain by keeping the Vietnamese at bay while not giving up Laos or Cambodia either. He did not have his father's indomitable personality, but he

continued the previous king's work by stimulating commerce and encouraging the revival of the arts. Under a state-held monopoly, the national income consisted of revenues acquired through the trade of goods with foreigners who had been allowed to open consulates in Bangkok. In 1820, the Portuguese were guaranteed the use of a plot of land on the river, in present-day Bush Lane, whereas the British were kept at a distance, as they threatened Thai control in the Malaysian Peninsula, although British and American missionaries were allowed to reside in the capital.

34 top left King Mongkut had a warm and charming personality. The portrait, painted in 1859, shows his fine and intelligent face, thoughtful eyes, curious mouth, and lean physique. The opulence of his clothing and hairstyle give the figure an aura of power, which the king wielded as a modern and enlightened monarch.

34 top right There are countries that by nature are multiethnic. Thailand has since time immemorial been populated by several ethnic groups: Thai, Mon, Khmer, Malay, Burmese, Karen, Meo, Akha, and Yao. This bill, issued by the Royal Treasury in 1853, states its value in eleven different languages, among which Chinese, Latin, and English.

In 1851, Mongkut Rama IV, the king most famous in the West – and the king featured in the film *Anna and the King* from the musical *The King and I* – ascended the throne. Completely different from the Hollywood character, portrayed as barbaric and a bit tyrannical, he was actually quite open, democratic for his time, and cultured, having had time to study during the long years in which, not being destined to take the throne, he lived at Wat Bowonnivet. He knew several classical languages, including Sanskrit and Latin, and spoke French and English. Besides the traditional sciences, he had studied history, mathematics, and astronomy. He loved scientific experimentation and understood the importance of new tech-

nologies, for which reason he began a program of modernization in the country. He introduced the telegraph, reformed the monetary and customs systems, and established a police force for domestic security. He enacted laws prohibiting families from selling girls as concubines or actresses and reduced the economic pressure on farmers. His decree forbidding the sale of opium was the first to be printed for public distribution. In his diplomatic dealings with foreign powers, he expressed himself in English or French, without the help of interpreters. At the palace, he founded the first modern school, in which Anna Lenowens was hired to teach, so that the king's wives and the princes could get an education.

His son, Chulalongkorn Rama V, who took the throne in 1868 still a minor, was able to prepare himself during his father's reign to face the problems presented during this period of maximum colonial expansion. The country was, in many aspects, still backward: its teak forests and mines were exploited without limits, the country's budget was not taking in enough revenues, bandits roamed the territory like the plague, and legal matters were decided by the whims of local princes. Upon reaching adulthood in 1874, he began his program of reforms, reorganizing the state's administration by creating ministries and a tax system, thus abolishing the crown's monopoly over foreign trade. Furthermore, he attempted to improve agricultural production by building irrigation canals. His influence was, however, fundamental in the field of culture: he founded public schools and universities that replaced the out-dated education system offered by the temples, and to create an intellectual and ruling class, he had the royal princes study abroad so that they could specialize in the sciences and advanced technologies. In 1897, he established a crown-funded foreign-study scholarship for the two best students to graduate from the high schools. He founded a museum and the National Library. To maintain the independence and integrity of the Thai territory during the frequent conflicts that arose with Western powers, he relinquished the Malaysian Peninsula, Laos, and Cambodia.

34-35 For many countries, especially in the East, steam-powered railways meant entrance into the modern era. In this photo, in Bangkok, the royal family attends the commencement of the railway's construction, which increasingly displaced the traditional systems of river transportation and ox-drawn carts.

After World War I, which saw Thailand at the side of the Allies, King Prajadhipok Rama VII had to facing the problems of financial crisis, the 1930s depression and the frustration of students who had received a Western education abroad now home, facing a backwardness not adequately resolved by the monarchy. With a bloodless coup d'état in June 1932, absolute monarchy ended, replaced by constitutional government. Following the abdication, as of 1935 the country was led by a regent's council that ruled until the crown prince, eight-year-old Ananda Mahidol reached adulthood. The period was characterized by conflict between the morally incompatible political forces of two brilliant leaders, united only by a common belief in the country's economic and social development.

They were lawyer Pridi Phanomyong, supported by intellectuals and students, and Luang Pibulsongkram, an army officer, supported by the military. First, Pridi set up an innovative and socially committed policy, but then in 1933, the conservative vision of Pibul, supported by Prime Minister Phya Phahol Phayuhasena, prevailed. In 1938, Pibul became prime minister, and in 1941, his authoritarian regime was forced to collaborate with the Japanese occupiers, while Pridi, supporting the Allies, entered the resistance. At the end of the war in 1946, with King Ananda Mahidol taking power, Pridi became prime minister. However, the king's sudden death brought Pibul back into power, which he held onto until 1957, when he was replaced by the general Sarit Thanarat. Khun

Sarit, a great man dear to Thai historical tradition, governed with dynamic energy until his death in 1963, launching the country on the road of economic development and political stability.

The figure of the king has maintained a stabilizing effect in the country's political situation, not lacking in social conflict. King Bhumibol Adulyadej Rama IX was born in 1927 in Cambridge, Massachusetts, where his father, Prince Mahidol of Songkla, studied medicine at Harvard University. He was crowned in Bangkok in 1950. With his presence, peaceful and steadfast, he has often prevented tensions between rivals from bursting into open conflicts. He demonstrates his authority above all by acting as a referee in internal disputes between the two poles of Thai political life, the military and the progressives, thus contributing to ensuring Thailand's democratic development. Much loved and respected above all for his ability to know and be close to his people, he has supported academic studies and commerce that have improved farming and livestock raising, environmental protection, and the social conditions of the ethnic minorities of the north. Like many Thai sovereigns, he is cultured and has an open and brilliant mind: with a degree in engineering, he is a musician, composer, painter, and photographer.

In 1950, he married his beautiful queen Sirikit Kitiyakara, with who he has had three children: the crown prince Vajiralongkorn and the princesses Maha Chakri Sirindhorn and Chulabhorn.

BANGKOK, CITY OF ANGELS

39 top left The
uniforms of the
soldiers look like those
of the English
"bobbies," but the
jacket is white, the
night stick has been
replaced by a sword,
and the helmet is
topped by a gold point.
Surrounded by the
exotic pavilions of the
Grand Palace of
Bangkok, the royal
guard performs the
change.

*38 In front of a
gracious Chinese-style
garden, the external
pavilions of the
Grand Palace of
Bangkok have
telescopic roofs covered
by green and ocher
tiles and gateways
surmounted by the
umbrella of the royal
insignia.*

*38-39 Behind the
enclosure walls of the
Grand Palace of
Bangkok, a forest
of spires and golden
pinnacles constitutes
the Wat Phra Keo
Complex, a summary
of Thai architectural
forms: octagonal-
based chedis,
phrangs, finger-
shaped spires, and
mongkuts, roofs of
decreasing-size discs
placed on a prasad,
a royal pavilion with
four pediments.*

Bangkok is the heart of Thailand, even though it is profoundly different from the rest of the country. A city that never fails to amaze, it is possible to return to it time and time again and never manage to unlock all of its secrets. When Taksin was elected king in 1768, Ayutthaya and its kingdom was nothing but a pile of ruins, and his first step on the road to reconstruction was to transfer the capital to Thonburi, on the banks of the Chao Phraya River. Not until Rama I ascended the throne did Bangkok, on the opposite side of the river, return to the light. First, fortifications and monasteries were built, and then in 1782, the Grand Palace (Phra Borom Maha Rajawang) was begun, which would become not only the royal residence but also the seat of government and the location of the royal chapel to hold the sacred image of the Emerald Buddha. Anxious to recreate the atmosphere of Ayutthaya, Rama I planned to build the palace in the bend of the river, on lands occupied by merchants and artisans, who, in order to go ahead with his project, were moved to Sampheng, present-day Chinatown. He then built a series of canals, the *khlong*, waterways that expand in a crescent shape across the urban area, giving the city the look of an Asian Venice. In this way, Bangkok truly looked like Ayutthaya, with the river, canals, myriad temples, and the city gates that were closed at dusk and reopened at dawn.

Although it is no longer the political and administrative center of Bangkok, the palace remains the city's spiritual nucleus. Surrounded by walls, it covers an area of about 1 sq. mile (2.6 sq. km) and is the best example of the Bangkok or Rattanakosin style, heir to the architectural tradition of Ayutthaya and enriched with Chinese and Western influences.

39 top right The prasad *is the building in which ceremonies tied to royalty and the state religion take place. It usually has a cruciform layout and is surmounted by an architectural element composed of discs of a decreasing size surmounted by a sharp spire. Royal funeral pyres have the* prasad *form.*

The complex is composed of an external court with the public buildings of the Ministry of Finance, from which one enters the enclosure of Wat Phra Keo, the Temple of the Emerald Buddha, at the entrance of which the 20-foot-high statues of *yaek* (demons) guard the way to the sacred place. Inside, are chapels and *chedi* (reliquary towers, or Thai-style *stupas*) and, on the eastern side, the eight *phrang* (Khmer-style towers) symbolizing the planets of Buddhist cosmology. The galleries, with paintings portraying stories from the *Ramayana*, border the central part of the temple's courtyard, where the Emerald Buddha's *bot* ('hall') stands, a chapel over 164 feet tall, surrounded by a portico of columns into which small tabernacles were interpolated. The multiple roof, able to support rather large architectural structures, ends in a point with a spiral, symbol of the *naga* serpent, and can shelter the meditating Buddha even when torrential rains slash the land for seven days. The *bot*'s triangular front pediment features entwining gold-enameled floral friezes and mosaics of mirrors in a thousand colors from which stands out the relief statue of Garuda, the god Vishnu's mount, whose image is again found in friezes on the base. Making the *bot*'s appearance even more brilliant, a series of small bronze bells fashioned into heart shapes hang from the ceiling, tinkling with every breeze. Thus, the peace is enlivened by silvery sounds, while the visitor's gaze in lost in a myriad of lights and colors. The interior decorations illustrate scenes from the life of Buddha and the *jataka* stories – more recent paintings in traditional style – done with the characteristically full and uniform brush strokes of color and with a sophisticated technique and masterly hand. The small statue of the Emerald Buddha, in reality a block of jasper of an extremely beautiful green color, measures about two feet tall and was found in 1436 at Chiang Mai inside another larger plaster statue, which broke in transport, revealing its precious contents. In 1778, King Taksin succeeded in bringing it back to Thailand. It is now preserved in a glass shrine topped by a pointed crown and surrounded by golden statues, and is dressed in precious garments changed each season by the king himself during a solemn ceremony.

40 Against a background of glass mosaic tesserae of a deep blue color, the volutes of the gold frieze stand out, located on the pediment of a building of Wat Phra Keo, the temple of the Emerald Buddha.

41 top left Long fangs poking out of their mouths characterize demons and warriors, as seen in this detail from wall paintings in a building of Wat Phra Keo in Bangkok.

41 top right The frescoes decorating the walls of temples illustrate episodes taken from the life of Buddha or from the Ramayana.

41 bottom left Multicolored relief mosaics decorate the walls of the Pantheon in the enclosure of the Grand Palace in Bangkok.

41 bottom right The entrance doors to the Wat Phra Keo Temple are guarded by the devaraja, the mythical kings of the cardinal points, known in Chinese mythology by the names of Ma, Zhao, Wen, and Li.

On a vast terrace north of the *bot* stand the buildings of the Prasad Phra Thepbidorn (Pantheon), the library, and the large golden *chedi*. The Pantheon has the shape of a *prasad*, one of the most characteristic constructions in Thai architecture: its body is covered by five overlapping multiple roofs, with orange tiles bordered with green, and is topped by a *phrang*. The mosaic covering the exterior walls, which in Thailand is prepared using ceramic, mirror, or porcelain tesserae, features a green and gold diamond-shaped motif. The building contains the statues of seven deceased kings of the Chakri dynasty and is opened every April 6, the anniversary of the dynasty's foundation. On the other hand, the memorial urns of the present-day royalty are found in Phra Nak, in the northern corner of the Wat Phra Keo enclosure. The library features a *mondop* structure, a square-shaped construction, often surrounded by columns and topped by a crown-shaped roof with several floors, culminating in an arrow-shaped spire. Inside, in a black-enamel shrine coated with mother-of-pearl, the *Tripitaka* is held, the Buddhist canon of the council proclaimed by Rama in 1805.

At the western edge of the terrace, north of the *bot*, there is the golden *chedi* of King Mongkut, in Ayutthaya style, covered with small gold leaves, a devotional custom widespread throughout Thailand. In the middle of the terrace, there is the model of Angkor Wat temple, a replica built by King Mongkut even before the complex was "discovered" in Cambodia, shrouded by the jungle, during the Nineteenth century.

44 top The Maha Dusit Prasad is the audience hall of the palace of Bangkok. A nine-level canopy symbolizing legitimate royalty hangs over the mother-of-pearl throne. The walls are decorated with a diamond pattern whereas the window frames are painted with trees and flowers.

44 bottom In the Chakri Residence, built by King Chulalongkorn, the throne room, Chakri Mahaprasad, is found, in which the king receives foreign ambassadors. Decorated in European 19th-century style, in the hall, the throne of inlaid silver covered by a white nine-level canopy stands out.

The internal courtyard, reachable from the external courtyard through a double gate, is the largest part of the palace with three groups of buildings: to the left, the Mahamontien, built by King Rama III, holds the Amarindra Hall once used for hearings, with its ancient boat-shaped throne; the Coronation Hall (Paisal Taksin); and the Chakrabardibhiman, the residence of the first three kings of the Chakri dynasty, in which the sovereign still spends the night after his coronation and in which the symbols of the royalty are held: the umbrella, crown, golden sword, flyswatter, and the golden shoes. In the west wing, gifts offered by foreign heads of state and other relics are on display.

The Chakrimahaprasad, King Chula-longkorn's residence, is an odd building built in 1882 and designed by an English architect who drew his inspiration from the Italian Renaissance, but on top of which, by express wish of the king, a Thai-style roof was added. Even the interior decoration of the rooms, which are currently used for official receptions and the presentation of credentials by foreign ambassadors, demonstrates a European flair. The large 19th-century pictures representing the Siamese foreign missions at the times of Louis XIV of France, Queen Victoria, and Napoleon III are intriguing.

Near the Chakrimahaprasad stands the Abhorn Pimok, a small pavilion that, in the past, served as the royal dressing room, for when the sovereign, before entering the Dusitmahaprasad, removed his crown and golden vestments as he descended from the palanquin. With the structure of a *prasad*, in pure Thai style, this little architectural gem combines all the characteristics of the Bangkok-Rattanakosin style.

The Dusitmahaprasad, one of the purest examples of Thai architecture, is a Greek-cross-shaped *prasad* with a multiple roof and royal-crown-shaped *phrang*, supported at the corners of its base by four statues of Garuda that sit on the roof. Built by Rama I in 1782 for coronation ceremonies, it contains the mother-of-pearl throne topped by a white canopy with nine tiers, symbol of the royalty. Since the coffin of King Rama I was displayed in this hall in 1809, it has been used only for this purpose. Next to the Mahamontien group, the Sivalaya Garden is bordered by buildings, such as the chapel of the Crystal Buddha, commissioned by King Chulalongkorn.

44-45 Built in 1882 by an English architect whose design, according to the fashion of the time, was inspired by the Italian Renaissance, the Chakri Residence was fitted with Thai-style roofs upon the express request of the king. Despite the obvious mixture of styles, the palace has a decisively majestic and pleasant appearance.

45 top A large Aubusson carpet on the floor, small Louis XV-style armchairs, and Empire chandeliers decorate the throne room of the Chakri Residence, in the Royal Palace of Bangkok, one of the rooms most highly marked by European influence. On the walls hang portraits of the kings of Thailand.

The palace complex faces the vast green lawn of the Sanam Luang Phramane, where the cremation ceremonies for members of the royal family took place. Around it stand the buildings of the Silkaporn and Thammasat universities, whereas on the western side of the square, there is the National Museum followed by the Wat Mahatat and then the National Library. The National Museum occupies the old buildings of the Wang Na Palace, built by Rama I for his brother, the "Second King," he who could succeed the king on the throne in the event of premature death. When Chulalongkorn eliminated the position in 1884, the palace was given over to be a museum, where today artifacts from the Ban Chiang culture and the historical periods of Thai art are on display, not to mention collections of royal palanquins, objects used in the theater arts and games, ceramics, ancient ivory pieces, mother-of-pearl, weapons, inscriptions, wooden sculptures, musical instruments, textiles, religious objects, and the carriages used in royal cremations.

In the gardens, the Buddhaisawan Chapel, built in 1787 to hold the Sukhothai-style 15th-century Phra Buddha Sihing, and the "Red House," once the private residence of Rama I's sister Princess Sri Sudarak, built in teak in the traditional style, can be visited.

46 top left Not far from the Royal Palace stands the National Museum, one of the most interesting in Southeast Asia. It includes the Buddhaisawan Chapel, a classic example of temple architecture of the Bangkok period.

46 center The Mon Dvaravati style, from the Indianized kingdom settled along the lower course of the Menam River, represents the initial phase of Thai sculpture. The Buddha Mon maintains the imprint of the classic beauty of Gupta art.

46 top right Built in 1795 to hold the statue of the valuable Phra Buddha Sihing, the Buddhaisawan Chapel has been embellished by a pediment with golden friezes. In the detail, the god Brahma mounts his ride, the goose Hamsa.

47 The stone statue of Ganesh belonged to the great island empire of Srivijaya, whose political influence extended as far as southern Thailand.

48 Sculpture in Thailand followed a evolutionary course that first felt the influence of Indian Gupta art and then learned the strength of the Khmer culture. This head from the National Museum of Bangkok demonstrates the Indian sensuality blended with majestic Khmer severity.

49 left This statue from the National Museum of Bangkok holds in the palm of its right hand the wheel, symbol of the eternal cycle of birth and rebirth. Buddha renounces Nirvana so that everyone can attain it and consents to be reborn continually, according to the wheel of samsara.

49 top right The National Museum of Bangkok has a variety of examples of sculpture from several Thai artistic periods and from all over Southeast Asia. This lovely sitting Buddha has been sculpted in high relief. The halo with the soft lines of Gupta sculpture culminates in a lotus bud.

49 bottom right Of clearly Cambodian influence, this statue in the National Museum of Bangkok features characteristics typical of the Angkor style. Sculpted from a single block of stone, in relief in front, it has an expressive impact that was created with just a few decisive lines.

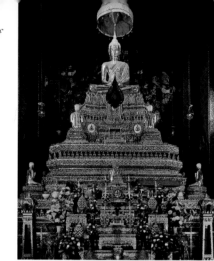

50-51 The complex of Wat Po occupies an 20-acre area and includes several buildings, among them a library, a Pali-language school, and the monks' residences. Rama III had it enlarged to include a school for the common people. The ancient school of Thai medicine at which medications and texts (even in English) are sold has its headquarters here.

South of the palace stands Wat Chetuphon, or Wat Po, the Temple of the Reclining Buddha, one of the biggest and oldest in the city and the headquarters of the school of traditional Thai medicine. Most likely built in the 16th century under the name of Wat Bodharam (the temple of the Bodhi tree), more than 70 small *chedi* decorated with pottery-shard mosaics, interspersed with miniature gardens, with four *viharn* ('sermon halls') at the cardinal points, line up around its double galleries. In the ambulatory that gives way to the internal courtyard sit the serene figures of a lovely series of Buddhas. The *bot* has elegant proportions and marble reliefs portraying scenes from the *Ramayana*, which are said to come from an Ayutthaya temple, but which more likely date back to the first half of the 1800s. Remarkable for their artistic and esthetic value, the window shutters on the *bot* are engraved and gilded, and the teak doors are lined with mother-of pearl. The main attractions at Wat Po are, however, its four *chedi*, covered with green, dark yellow, and blue mosaics, and the Viharn Phra Non with the big statue of the reclining Buddha, made of molded stucco bricks and covered with gold plate. The position symbolizes his journey to Nirvana, and the bottom of his feet bear the 108 sacred signs characteristic of the Buddha. In the courtyards, there are statues of mythical figures, merchants, soldiers, and ladies-in-waiting donated by the Chinese as votive offerings, and turtles swim in a well surrounded by strange stones.

50 left Wat Po is the oldest temple in the Thai capital. Located south of the Royal Palace, it holds an enormous statue of the Reclining Buddha covered with plaster and sheets of gold leaf, measuring 151 feet long and 49 feet high. On the soles of its feet, the 108 signs that make it possible to identify the true Buddha have been inlaid.

50 top right Made up of several chedis and viharns, the Wat Po, whose real name is Wat Chetuphon, was built in the 16th century under the name of Wat Bodharam, the temple of the tree of bodhi, from which the popular name of Wat Po is supposedly derived. In one of the chapels, the statue of Buddha shines, entirely gilded, upon the tall throne.

51 top left Wat Po is particularly dear to members of the Chinese community. The courtyard is decorated with beautiful statues given by Chinese as votive offerings or as philanthropic donations by which to gain merit.

51 top right Many ceramic tiles cover the chedi *and* phrang *of Wat Po. Recent restoration has returned its porcelain decorations to splendor, removing its run-down look of the past.*

The Wat Traimit Temple is known for its Sukhothai-style solid-gold statue of Buddha, over eleven feet tall and weighing over five tons, which was discovered when the layer of stucco concealing it accidentally broke. Wat Traimit is in the middle of Chinatown, the city's most lively and entertaining section, with tree-lined avenues, low houses, and street-level shops. Everything is sold here, from food, to furniture, to funeral accessories, to anything needed to make offerings to monks. Chinatown never closes and never stops, because the Chinese sleep in the rooms above the shops open to the street, where they spend their day, work, eat when they are hungry, and raise their children. Hiding in a labyrinth of ancient alleys, in the heart of a neighborhood teeming with life, the Kuan Choi Khan Temple is a little secret oasis for the worship of family ancestors and Taoist divinities. Here, in a charming Chinese-style buding, inside which open ancient courtyards and closed doors made of old-perfumed wood, in the shadows and silence, among clouds of incense, Guan Yin of Mercy wraps the faithful – old Chinese men in traditional dress, young expectant mothers, students, and men asking for luck in their business – in his serene gaze.

At night, when no one is buying anything, the streets fill with flowers: under the lamplight run by generators, along the streets and in front of the shops, orchid, jasmine, daisy, and rose sellers pop up. The blossoms sell for next to nothing in this flower market in the middle of a city that seems to belong the future, tinted by their brilliant colors, filled with their scent, only to vanish at the first light of dawn, giving way to the morning traffic.

53 top right *Those who want to eat anything whatsoever and at any hour should go to Bangkok's Chinese quarter. Small restaurants, corner kiosks, shops, or simple carts with a steaming pot offer the most exquisite foods in Asian cuisine.*

Continuing south, the visitor comes to a square featuring the enormous red structure of a giant seesaw. No one can clearly explain its purpose or what it signifies. Wat Suthat, with its *bot* whose walls are entirely covered by gorgeous paintings illustrating the life of Buddha, looks onto the square. Wat Bowonniwet, on Phrasumane Road, northeast of the National Museum, is where King Mongkut resided for fourteen years and founded the Dhammayukti sect. In the *bot* towers the Phra Buddha Jinasiha, one of the most beautiful Sukhothai-style sculptures.

Proceeding toward the river along Phrasumane Road, the visitor arrives at the river and at an odd hexagonal-shaped building: it is the Phrasumane Tower with its ancient fortifications whose semicircle outline can be identified by following the Khlong Bang Lampu as far as the Mahakan fortress and then continuing along the Khlong Ong Ang, which ends in the Chao Phraya at the Phra Pok Klao Bridge. The riverbank hides a host of surprises: after the highly modern skyscraper containing Rivercity, an entire shopping mall of Thai and Burmese antiques, there is the sophisticated colonial-style Oriental Hotel, where it is worth stopping to enjoy an English-style cup of tea as was done a century ago. Tiny Bush Lane carries one back in time to the era of the East India Company, even though its white-shuttered buildings no longer contain exotic goods, but rather the most expensive boutiques and jewelry shops in Southeast Asia.

On the opposite side of the river, the tranquil panorama of Thonburi, the original city center, is dominated by the elegant form of the *phrang* of Wat Arun, the Temple of Dawn, easily reached by a ferry ride. The 282-foot-tall *phrang* represents Mount Meru, the mythical center of the universe, the home of the gods, and the symbol of the spiritual path to enlightenment. The upper floors rest on a square base and gradually step, decreasing in size, back toward the top. From the base, a staircase climbs as far as the residence of Indra on his mount, Erawan, the three-headed elephant that looks out from a niche just under the point of the *phrang*. Each level features a balustraded walkway for ritual ambulation and the upper level is supported by a series of statues of Devada, Yaksha, and Ling (monkeys), the mythical creatures that inhabit Mount Meru. The *phrang* is entirely covered with porcelain chips in floral patterns that sparkle in the sun, brightening the dark of night. Originally founded as Wat Cheng, the palace chapel, by King Taksin after he moved the capital to Bangkok, it was reoccupied by monks and owes its present-day appearance to the reconstruction project begun under Rama II in 1792 and completed under Rama III. The monks of Wat Arun enjoy the privilege of receiving their yellow robes from the king, which are handed over during the festival of Thot Kathin.

58 top Scooters, cars, knots of people, and the façades of the houses look like a circus of advertisement billboards. This is one of many streets full of life, shops, and traffic to be found in downtown Bangkok.

58 bottom Once the area between the main arteries of downtown was one of the city's more exclusive neighborhoods, then, traffic threatened to suffocate it. To survive, Rajadamri Road was given a second, elevated roadway.

The futuristic version of Bangkok stretches beyond Khlong Phadung Krungkasem along the great avenues that radiate toward the city outskirts. Praram IV Road runs from the Bangkok train station with its 19th-century iron-vaulted ceiling to the Pasteur Institute, where antidotes for snake venom are prepared and, in Saladaeng Circle, to the immense four-sided lawn of Suan Lumpini, the largest park in the city, with ponds and the statue of King Mongkut that watches over the artistic activities of school children and health enthusiasts out for a jog. The parallel streets of Praram I, Ploenchit, Sukhumvit, and New Phetburi are just as crowded, chaotic, traffic-jammed, polluted, and entertaining as can be imagined.

58-59 The velvet blue of the night lights up with a thousand lights. The river becomes a mirror, the skyscrapers take on the look of glowing arcs, the streets are like stars shooting toward the outskirts of the city, and in the parks along the river people have candlelit dinners by the swimming pool. All this happens in the panorama of Bangkok by night.

59 The colors of the sunset reveal the burning line of Rama VIII Bridge, surrounded only by the silence of the waters of the Menam Chao Praya River. The sunset silences even the noise of the boats in the river harbor.

60 top left Many years ago, between Rachadamri and Ploenchit Road, there was a small shrine bearing the image of Erawan, the mythical three-headed elephant that is said to bring good luck. Still today, people bring offerings of jasmine necklaces for good luck, and the small shrine is always buried under flowers.

60 top right To gain merit, it is necessary to do good deeds, such as making donations. Near Wat Suthat, on Bamrungmuang Road, shops sell religious articles: statues of all sizes, incense, and kits for monks containing cloth for their robe, a bowl, tall candles, and even detergent, all in a plastic pail.

60-61 To solve the traffic problem, the Sky Train, the elevated metropolitan transport system, was born. Even if the more standard subway system is available, the "Sky" is more fun. From above, it is possible to discover the green lawns of the Royal Golf Club, hidden gardens, and flowering rooftop terraces, and all for the price of a train ticket.

The elevated transportation system makes an exciting ride through the Bangkok panorama: the city, reveals its secrets both small and large. Along Rachadamri, across from embassies and chic hotels, appear the green oases of golf clubs. The visitor sees super-tall daringly modern buildings, where steel and glass abound, still infiltrated by the old, low houses of traditional neighborhoods, their terraces guarded by iron bars covered with tropical plants, or the traditional houses and small temples in green gardens. At the entrance of the most expensive skyscrapers, as at the door of the simplest houses, a miniature house for the spirit of the place, as ornate as a temple or as plain as a wooden dwelling, is never lacking: none is without offerings of flowers and incense. The panorama sparkles with its mirrored windows, but also thanks to the golden tiles of the temples or the silvery domes of the mosques, whereas a touch of gray reveals the presence of a little cathedral in mock Gothic style. Climbing the stairs to one of the downtown stations, thousands of surprises can be found among the shops selling everything possible, the cafés, bars, and restaurants serving foods from around the world. Walking among the indescribable confusion of vendors, beggars, and passers-by, there is, however, behind the best shopping arcades, a corner with a little silver-mirrored tabernacle for Erawan: he is said to bring luck, so the skyscrapers step aside to leave him space so that he may receive the offerings of yellow and fuchsia flowers from those asking for success and happiness.

61 For getting around town, the Taxi-Meters are a good deal, they have efficient meters, and are air conditioned. At rush hour, you can take all the time you want to admire the panorama while sitting comfortably and cool, as traveling times prolong considerably.

Otherwise, there is the tuk-tuk, the heir to the rickshaw, a scooter with a seat for two behind the driver. The price is similar to that of the taxis, but it is certainly more fun, as the driver, often wearing white gloves, squeezes quickly through the cars stuck in traffic.

Behind the futuristic World Trade Center – a monument to modern consumerism – in the traffic, with the tracks of the trains that streak above the visitor's head, and taking care not bump into cripples or the band of blind people begging for money, the visitor finds the entrance to an old Thai-Chinese temple. Cats and dogs basking in the sun inhabit its courtyard, an ancient world of peace and quiet with old *chedi* whose plaster is humidity-stained and little well-kept gardens. Anyone finding an abandoned puppy brings it to the monks who will adopt it, and it is common to see worshippers adding canned and dry food and leftovers for their four-legged friends to the food and clothes they bring to the bonzes.

The liveliest street in Bangkok is Sukhumvit, both by day and night. During the day, it is crowded with shops and stalls; at night, it is lit by the lights of the bars, restaurants, and massage parlors. Adventure is close at hand, but also entertainment and games, to complete a cheerful evening spent in the deep blue nights tinted by the signs of a thousand colors.

62 top left Every day old buildings die and new ones quickly take their place. In the side streets, people continue to live in rather old houses, with electricity poles bearing tangles of wires.

62 top right In the luxurious hotels of Bangkok, the impeccable service is still that which visitors received in the past. On the terrace of the Peninsula Hotel on the river, having breakfast, and dinner are special experiences.

62 bottom The World Trade Center: in its arcades are haute-couture shops, sports equipment, CDs and DVDs, books, objects of design, and handmade items. Then, there are bars and restaurants of all kinds selling Thai foods.

63 In the evening, the bars and clubs light up. Having fun is assured, no matter what one's tastes, and the signs, wink and hint at the surprises the night may hold...

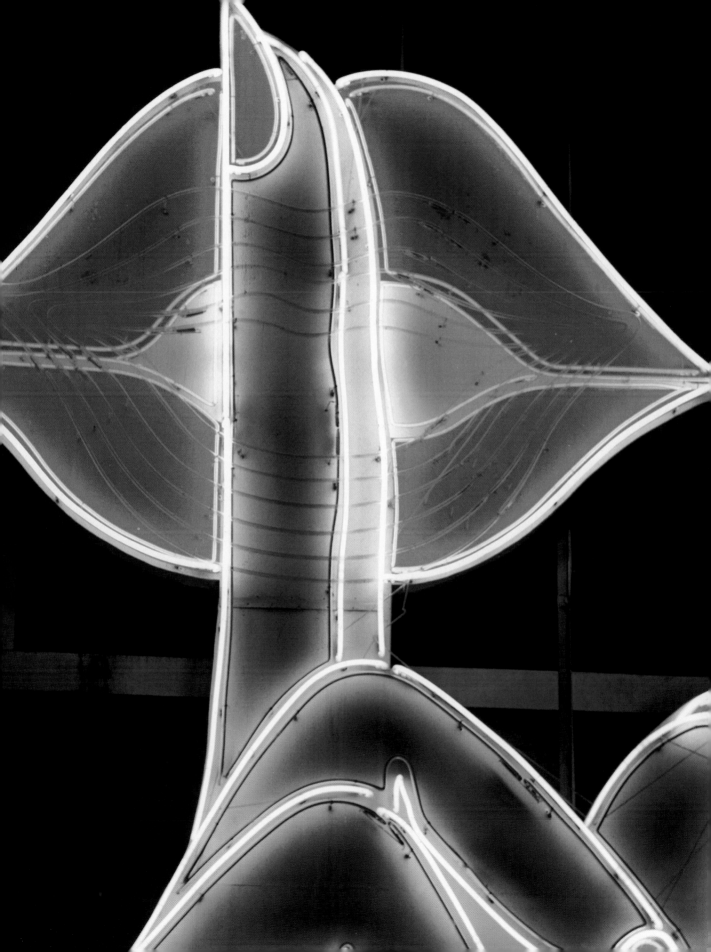

64 top Located near Phraram I, the museum-house of Jim Thompson is an intact taste of old Bangkok. The doors of the living room open onto the terrace looking onto Khlong San Sap. The furnishings include classical Thai pieces, low colonial-era armchairs, and Western table lamps.

64 bottom In the garden of Suan Pakkard, a pavilion from the old Wat Ban Kling, on Chao Praya outside Bangkok, has been reassembled. The walls covered with paintings in black and gold lacquer may have been done in Ayutthaya. Even the paintings are of fantastic quality.

Behind a modern and chaotic façade, the little treasures of the past hide themselves. Looking onto Khlong Sam Sap, sunk into the tropical vegetation of a romantic garden, is what was the residence of Jim Thompson, the American who revolutionized design in the Thai silk industry during the years after World War II. It is said that he was a spy, perhaps because he disappeared into nothing during a trip in Burma. The fact is that he invented a style of life based on his love for Thai art. His house is made up of a group of different traditional teak structures, on stilts, that together form a delightful living space, decorated with locally handmade objects and textiles. Jim Thompson was a collector of curiosities, but to see real antiques and art in the interior decoration of a traditional home, it is necessary to visit the Suan Pakkard Palace, once the residence of Princess Chumbot Nagara Sgarva. Upon entering its garden, one encounters the Thailand of two centuries ago, with the lovely dark-wood houses, the library pavilion of an old temple, and a pond. Inside, the antique decoration is embellished with art miniatures, wooden sculptures, archeological finds, dolls, and classical-theater costumes. It is a dip in the past, where the house's magical atmosphere is increased by the curious effect of a crystal skyscraper rising toward the sky that stands just behind the garden enclosure wall.

64-65 *At the end of World War II, the American Jim Thompson fell in love with Thailand and its silk. He managed to revive its production to the point that the "Jim Thompson" brand name supplied the stylists of Paris. His house's living room displays his love for Thai art. The decoration incorporates traditional elements that have been Westernized.*

65 top *Isolated from the metropolis and inserted into a garden out of the past, the Suan Pakkard Museum was the home of the princes Chumbot Negara Svarga, composed of traditional houses connected by walkways. The rooms are furnished with valuable objects and house the princess' collection of objet d'art.*

Speaking of magic, along the highly trafficked Soi Sukhumvit 2, after the Asok fruit and vegetable market, behind a white wall, hides the Siam Society, founded in 1904 and sponsored by the future king Rama VI in order to study and promote interest in the arts, architecture, and the environment of Thailand. In 1963, Nang Kimhaw Nimmanhaeminda donated Kamthieng House to the organization, a splendid example of Lanna architecture, built in 1848 on the banks of the Ping River in Chiang Mai by Lady Mae Saed, a descendant of Prince Muang Chae. Kamthieng is now the ethnological museum of the cultures of the north. Daily life in a Lanna case was conditioned by the interaction of people, the place, and the spirits, be-

cause respect for the visible as well as invisible forces of nature was also a way to honor ancestors and the collective memory. Passed down from the mother to the daughter, it is said that the spirits of three sisters who once lived there still inhabit the house today. Many stories are told about the mysterious apparitions of ladies wearing traditional northern clothing and strange and unexplainable events have been reported in the house.... What does it matter if in front of the house, the chaos of the traffic and skyscrapers is everywhere? They do not cover the sky, and the arcane presences can live alongside the men of today, to remind them that there is no past or future, but only a long continuous wheel turning in the immensity of time.

68-69 Sunset is the best time of day to admire the ruins of Sukhothai. The ancient statues and the outline of the pagodas are silhouetted against the rosy light, awaiting the shadows, and they speak of the history and the splendor of the past.

69 top left On a brick platform, the towers of Wat Mahathat Sukhothai have been preserved as prescribed by the original concept of a Khmer-style temple. The placement of the towers at the cardinal points corresponds to cosmological theory, with the central phrang *representing Mount Meru, the axis of the world.*

Thailand is shaped like an elephant head, with Bangkok located near the mouth and tusks. The trunk extends beyond Thai territory into the Malaysian Peninsula, the farming regions of the northeast near the Mekong River occupy the ears, and Chiang Mai sits on the head, the capital of the north, ringed by mountains where the Yao, Karen, and Meo tribes reside.

North of Bangkok extend the central plains, flat regions of rice paddies and tropical plantations, and almost smack in the middle in the vicinity of Pitsanuloke, there is the ancient city of Sukhothai. The ruins are reached by crossing a park of centuries-old trees, including acacias, breadfruit trees, and frangipani. After passing the moats and earthworks, Wat Mahathat appears against a background of palm trees. According to an ancient belief, planting a group of trees brought luck, and Rama Kamhaeng, Suhkothai's greatest king, endowed the great square in which his people gathered to attend ceremonies with a thick bunch of palms. When the moon was full or it was a new moon, the king, riding an elephant, went to the Aranyk Monastery outside the city to collect his thoughts in meditation, and his people gathered to watch the court procession from this palm-shaded square. The capital's splendor can be imagined from the ruins: all the buildings are of an impressive size, and yet their shapes are never squat or heavy but rather elegant, with simple and soft lines.

68 Indian culture spread throughout Southeast Asia. Some sculptures at Wat Mahathat have the opulent forms and fabulous jewels of original models. The position of the hands, derived from Sanskrit texts, is found unchanged in classic Thai dances.

69 top right The hand gesture of the Buddha in Wat Mahathat at Sukhothai is named bhumisparsa mudra, which indicates the moment of enlightenment in Buddhist iconography. The hands with their fingertips pointed slightly upward resemble lotus buds about to blossom.

70 top left Against the background of a large chedi in the style imported from Sri Lanka, the Buddha of Wat Sra Sri in Sukhothai sits in the pan man wichai position with his hands in the bhumisparsa mudra position. The statue stands out among six rows of octagonal columns. Opposite stands the bot reflected in pool of water lilies.

70 top right The stupa of Sri Lanka becomes more slender and taller in the Sukhothai style. The chedi of Wat Sra Sri is composed of two overlapping hemispheres separated by a triple circle of rings, with a three-floored harmika supporting the needle-like pinnacle. Despite its simple lines, the chedi has proportions of great elegance.

70-71 The Eastern artist recreates his subject after lengthy observation, until he is able to reproduce only what his mind has retained. If the subject is Buddha, meditation allows the artist to express Buddha's essence. The statue of Wat Si Chum at Sukhothai bears traces of the gold plating offered as a sign of devotion on its fingernails and hands.

71 The massive structure of the mondop of Wat Si Chum is striking. A triangular cross-section of the wall reveals, but not entirely, the most splendid statue in Sukhothai, Phra Buddha Achana, from the second half of the 14th century and just over 48 feet tall. Inside, Buddha appears squeezed between the roofless walls, with the flame atop his head pointing to the sky.

The Sukhothai architectural style, the first authentically Thai one, is characterized by chedis, the reliquary stupa of Indian origin, in the shape of a lotus bud, placed on a two-floored base, the first of which is surrounded by statues of elephants and the second decorated with niches containing illustrations.

Wat Mahatat is the largest of the temples and has a mighty, square foundation from which rise the columns of the bot, the chedi, the four axial Khmer-style towers, and the four Srivijaya-style brick towers, with their cube-shaped form, niches, and a circular chedi. From the variety of styles featured in the monuments, it can be understood that Sukhothai was a cosmopolitan society, with Mon, Khmer, and Thai inhabitants who produced art of exquisite elegance. Among small streams and umbrella-shaped trees rise the phrangs with their beautiful geometric decorations, a centuries-old Bodhi tree whose roots extend over the lawn, and the big bell-shaped chedi of Wat Sra Sri. Its lovely statue of Buddha is reflected in the water among chopped-off columns and nymphs as it looks toward the bot, floating in the middle of a pond.

"A big house does not make for greatness, a small house can hold a big heart. The heart is important not the house." Thus say the Thai, and it may be out of this belief that the habit of erecting extremely tall statues of Buddha and then enclosing them in the tight space of small mondops, chapels for images, was born. They can be seen from far away, because by now the cabin no longer has its roof so the head sticks up above the walls, its serene gaze falling onto empty space. The most spectacular of these apparitions is in Wat Si Chum: from the diamond-shaped cut in the wall, the enormous, smiling face of Buddha can be glimpsed, with his eyes benevolently looking down on men, who can barely reach his fingers, and only small white-and-black-winged birds manage to gracefully land on the bun in his hair. Not far away, a chedi with an elegant arrow-shaped spire is supported by a row of elephants whose heads and trunks have been miraculously saved from destruction by the invading armies of the past.

Si Satchanalai is another archeological site with a magical atmosphere, hidden in the dense folds of the tropical vegetation. The city, close to the borders of the kingdom of Sukhothai, was the northernmost rest stop (*dharmasala*) in the Khmer road network, which Jayavarman VII had built to connect Angkor Thom to the outlying regions. The most beautiful building at Si Satchanalai is Wat Chang Lom, which dates back to the time of Rama Kamhaeng, with its square, two-floor base. Natural size elephant statues surround the first level, whereas the second is decorated with niches containing statues of Buddha. The semi-ruined statues of the elephants reveal a brilliant construction technique: at first sight, they seem to have been sculpted in stone, a material not readily available in the region, but they are actually made of bricks covered in plaster, in which the figure was shaped and the details defined. The *chedi*, shaped like a bell, rests on the second floor of the structure, with its bare bricks and plaster now crumbling and blackened by the humidity. Its restoration could not accomplish more to undo the assaults of time, but this only serves to increase the charm of these ancient blocks.

72 Compared to the original model of the Mahatupa dagoba at Anuradhapura (Sri Lanka), the bell-shaped chedi of Wat Chang Lom in Sukhothai is more elegant. The chedi rises from a quadrangular base with niches, from which stick out elephant heads. The dome, the harmika, the pinnacled spire, and the elephants are in brick, once covered by stucco. The niches of the next floor up hold statues of Buddha.

73 left Rigid forms and a squared-off build characterize the statues located in the niches of Wat Chang Lom at Sri Satchanalai. The statues of Buddha are often covered with orange scarves offered by worshippers.

73 right The only surviving monument from the Rama Kamhaeng period, Wat Chang Lom was built for the sacred relics of Maha Datu, previously in Wat Mahathat of Chalieng, as attested to by a 1285 inscription.

The capital of the north is Chiang Mai, founded in 1296 by Mengrai. Though it is the second-largest city in Thailand, it has preserved a peaceful and traditional look. Of the fortifications, built in 1796 by King Taksin, only the moat remains to, along with the city gates (built in later years), delimit the outline of the ancient city. Neighborhoods and suburbs are crowded with the workshops of artisans producing lacquered objects, niello-decorated silver, painted umbrellas, and the ethnic fabrics of the northern tribes. The temples and monasteries are in Lanna style, characterized by imposing multiple roofs and tripartite façades sumptuously decorated with sculpted wood. The oldest temple in Chiang Mai is Wat Chiang Man, built in 1292. Wat Phra Singh features a library pavilion on a tall brick base, with abundant decorations in wood, glass mosaics, and stuccoes. Wat Jet Yot is a model of the Mahabodi Temple in Bodhgaya, India, whereas Wat Chedi Luang has preserved its big *chedi*, although damaged by an earthquake, with its base supported by elephants and its staircases adorned with *naga*. However, the temple that best represents the spirit of the city is Wat Doi Suthep, on a hill dominating the city. It is reached by a 290-step staircase lined by long *naga* serpents that form a balustrade and that, at the base of the stairs, raise their heads in defense of the sacred place against evil spirits. At the top, a big golden angular *chedi* in Burmese style dominates the valley. To the east, the region's history is more modern.

74 top Lan Na architecture features downward sloping telescopic roofs and tripartite façades sumptuously decorated with carved wood. The Viharn Lai Kham of Wat Phra Singh, built between 1806 and 1809 as prescribed by the classic canons of the Lan Na style, has its entrance watched over by Naga serpents and Burmese lions.

74 center Of Burmese tradition, a taste for gold in the architectural decoration characterizes the interior of Wat Phra Singh in Chiang Mai, whose original nucleus was built in 1345. In 1545, representatives of the Lan Na Kingdom gathered here to elect Prince Jetta of Luang Prabang king.

74 bottom The interior of the viharn *of Wat Phra Singh, in Chiang Mai, is decorated with Burmese-style wall murals in which the characters are portrayed each with their own particular and unconventional individual facial features. This example depicts the story of the prince and the golden shell.*

75 Situated in the old center of Chiang Mai, the chedi of Wat Phra Singh is the oldest and most important in the city. It was built in 1345 by King Pa Yo of Lan Na to house the ashes of his father. It is composed of overlapping circular floors that recede as they go higher, with its pinnacle gold plated at the base and top.

76 In the convent of Wat Jet Yot in the outskirts of Chiang Mai, next to the monks' quarters, large golden statues are covered by the traditional orange robes. The Reclining Buddha is considered that of Tuesday, the upright Buddha protects those born on Sunday, whereas the one on the right, with the donations plate, is that of Wednesday.

77 Wat Chiang Man, built in 1292, is the oldest temple in Chiang Mai. Among the teak columns, a large golden Buddha stands in the background of a copy of the Buddha Sila, the original of which came here in 1290. Together with the Phra Buddha Sae Tang Tamani, in quartz crystal, it supposedly has the power to make it rain.

78-79 From above, the view encompasses the perspective entirety of Wat Doi Suthep, in Chiang Mai. The octagonal chedi, covered in golden copper, reveals Burmese stylistic traits: an angled base, a structure that grows progressively narrower toward the top, and a golden railing delimiting the sacred corridor. The chedi is surrounded by viharns placed at the cardinal points.

79 top left Until recent times, there existed only one steep path leading to Wat Phra Doi Suthep, located seven miles away from Chiang Mai on a mountain 3,245 feet high. Only in 1934 was an access road built to the 290-step stairway that leads to the temple's platform. At the sides of the staircase, the banisters are shaped like seven-head Naga serpents.

79 top right In front of the big chedi with the golden umbrellas, worshippers prostrate themselves in prayer on the bare marble floors during the celebration of Makha Bucha, in commemoration of the 1,250 disciples who gathered to listen to the words of Buddha. To gain merit, they recite mantras holding little incense sticks between their joined hands.

78 In the corners of the ambulatory in the chedi of Wat Phra Doi Suthep, next to the four viharn, the copper umbrellas, characteristic of northern Thai sanctuaries, look like they are made from gold-plated crochet. The little side altars are always adorned with flowers, little candles, and sticks of votive incense.

80 top left Inside Wat Suan Dok, in Chiang Mai, which in the 14th century was the garden of King Kuna, one of the largest and most beautiful bronze sculptures of Thai art is found. It is the Buddha Phra Chao Tue, whose soldering was completed around 1504.

80 top right Although it is not one of the most important temples in Chiang Mai, it is definitely one of the most charming: Wat Puak Hong, on Samlan Road dates back to the 17th century and shows, above all in its exterior decorations, ample traces of Chinese influences.

80-81 In 1370, King Kuna built a chedi to hold part of the relics of the monk Phra Maha Sumana (the other part is found in Wat Doi Suthep) at Wat Suan Dok, outside the ancient city's walls. Around the main chedi, the funereal chedis of the princely family of Chiang Mai were erected from 1907 on.

81 left It is said that the king of the Nagas, Mucalinda, either a serpent or dragon of great wisdom, offered shelter to Buddha by covering him with his cobra head and enveloping his body with his coils. In his honor, he is positioned to guard temples, like the Nagas that decorate the stairways of Wat Suan Dok.

81 top right Wat Puak Hong displays the typical structure of a circular-tower chedi with decorated niches. On its upper terraces, parts of its original stucco paintings have been preserved in good condition.

81 bottom right Rising from a terraced platform, the bell-shaped chedi of Wat Suan Dok, in Chiang Mai, features a somber elegance, animated by the *arches of the gateways and a series of smaller stupas. The terraces are connected, at the four cardinal points, by staircases with railings in the form of Naga serpents.*

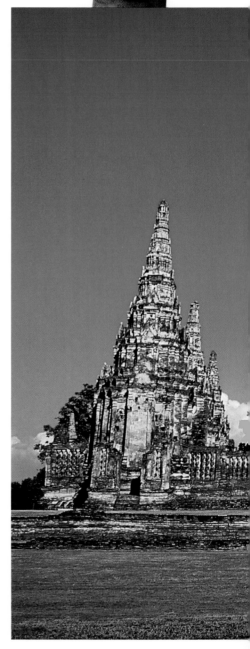

On the river 45 miles from Bangkok, Ayutthaya is a peaceful provincial city with low buildings that look out from palm groves and frangipani standing next to *chedi*s, *phrang*s, and statues, which are a bit crooked, a bit broken, and in the classical style enriched with Khmer and Mon elements.

The *chedi* of Ayutthaya is composed of a molded base from which rises its bell-shaped body. At the cardinal points, the door of the sanctuary and three niches feature avant-corps like little temples with pointed roofs. The spire elongates in a decorative motif of layered rings and rests on a columned ambulatory. The stones blackened with time bear signs of devotion: the statues – even the 30-foot-long one of the Buddha having reached Nir-vana that lies in a forest clearing – are wrapped in the monks' saffron-colored swathes of fabric, and a stone head entangled in the roots of a giant banyan tree looks out serenely from perfumed clouds of votive incense.

On the Chao Phraya River, in a bend where the waters slow their pace and flatboats proceed solemnly, Wat Chai-wathanaram seems to watch over the river with its fluted-columned *phrang*, its towers covered with empties niches, and its chipped *chedi* next to a breadfruit tree. The statues with their wise and severe appearance turn their gaze to the water, the yellow and orange flash of their shoes standing out against the antique red of the bricks and the dirty white of the stuccoes.

87 top left Built by
King Rama Thibodi
in 1353, close to his
first residence,
Wat Buddhaisawan
is one of the oldest
monasteries in
Ayutthaya.
The ancient buildings
are hidden by the
modern viharn, whose
interior shines with
golden statues.

86 top The chedi of
Wat Yai Chai
Mongkol is the first
visible monument in
the archaeological area
of Ayutthaya. It was
built in 1592 by King
Naresuen to
commemorate his
victory in a duel
against a Burmese
general.

86 bottom Statues of
Buddha in a line and
ancient gestures of
devotion are seen at
Wat Yai Chai Hongron
in Ayutthaya. The gold
covers the stone and its
reflection illuminates
the mind of the
worshipper. The sheet of
pure gold will earn the
girl some merit.

86-87 According to
tradition, the remains
of the first king of
Ayutthaya were
cremated here. Probably
erected in 1369 by King
Ramesuen, Wat Phra
Ram has an elegant
phrang with stucco
paintings of Garuda,
Nagas, and mythical
figures in action.

87 top center
In 1424, king Boromaraja dedicated Wat Rajaburana, in Ayutthaya, to his brothers, killed in a duel. A frescoed crypt hid gold tablets and figurines. The courtyard has several chedi.

87 top right As in Khmer-style temple constructions, the cella of the phrang is accessed through any of four doors in niches located at the cardinal points. The phrang of Wat Rajaburana has statues of Buddha sculpted on the doors of the niches.

88 top Thanks to restorations, the temple of Phimai, near Nakhon Ratchasima, has returned to its original splendor. The entire complex dates back to the end of the 11th century.

88 center Phimai has a harmonious appearance, as well demonstrated by the perfection of its tower.

88 bottom Farmers of the south usually use buffaloes in their work. In the province of Mae Hong Son though, they prefer to use a cow with an adipose hump.

89 In the mountain chains of the north, the rivers Ping, Wang, Yom, and Nan run in a southerly direction and then flow together into the Menam, whose name means "big water."

The regions of the northeast, once underdeveloped, feature a rich and evocative landscape of well-farmed rice paddies surrounded by palm, tamarind, and mango trees. On the horizon, the mountains are covered with teak woods, and in the villages with their lovely old houses, the traditional social fabric and serene country wisdom have been maintained. Animals are the friends of man, and when roosters, cows, buffalos, or dogs cross the street, the cars slow down to avoid them. The cultural characteristics are prevalently Khmer, and the temples, even if they are not as impressive as those at Angkor, possess a delicate grace and boast pretty reliefs exquisitely executed in pink sandstone. The temple of Phimai is a jewel, however small, because, according to the Thai, human sacrifices were not demanded for its construction, at once harmonious and proportioned, sumptuous but not excessive.

90 top left The entrance to the antechamber of the main sanctuary of Prasat Phnom Rung near Ta-pek, in Buriram Province, is watched over by an imposing dvarapala, a sandstone door-guarding sentinel, whose figure of massive proportions with a face bearing Cambodian features reveals its Khmer origin.

90 top right Shiva Natyaraja, the god of destruction necessary to make reincarnation possible, dances in the lovely relief situated over the lintel of the main sanctuary's antechamber.

90 bottom left All the main parts of the temple were built at the beginning of the 12th century, during the reign of the king of Angkor, Suryavarman II. However, the site was already considered sacred by the mid-10th century.

Prasat Phnom Rung, between Nakhon Ratchasima (Korat) and Surin, is the most beautiful of the Khmer temples in Thailand. A sanctuary dedicated to Shiva, it was built between the 10th and 12th centuries on an extinct volcano located south of Angkor, rather than to the east as was customary. A series of staircases lead to the first platform. The second level consists of a 66-foot-long paved way ending in another staircase that rises until a bridge with *naga* serpents, whose crowned heads lift from the baluster. Finally, a final series of four steep ramps leads to the open space of the main sanctuary, which is reflected in the lotus-flower-covered waters of two pools, sym-bols of the cosmic sea of creation. The wall that encloses the central area of the sanctuary is formed by a closed gallery, blocked at the cardinal points by the gate-ways to the sacred area, in the form of lit-tle cruciform temples, preciously decorat-ed with *phrang* domes.

The main sanctuary rests on a based sculpted with lotus petals and diamonds and is towered over by a five-floor *phrang* completely covered with sculptures por-traying *naga*, *rishi*, and gods. The reliefs that cover the doorjambs, the corners, the lintels, and the pediments of the sanctu-ary and the galleries are splendidly made, finely sculpted with the history of stone as told by Hindu mythology.

90 bottom right The entrance of the main sanctuary is dominated by the most delicate reliefs in Prasat Phanom Rung. A head of Kala, a mythical animal, looms over two parrots looking at each other, surrounded by floral motifs.

91 The main phrang of Prasat Phanom Rung, in the middle of the monastery, features a platform with lotus-petal and diamond sculptures and an internal cella. Its pyramidal roof has gables and antefixes decorated with reliefs.

92-93 Originating in China and flowing down through Laos, the historic Mekong River follows the Thai border east of the province of Ubon Ratchathani. The region, isolated in the past, is now blooming with agricultural activity thanks to the construction of dams and the draining of the swamps.

93 top Its foundations date back to the 9th century and it is one of the most holy sacred places in the northeast: the temple Wat Phra That of That Phanom. The present-day temple is modern, but the chedi, *with its peculiar cruet shape, is very old. It has been recently restored.*

The territory that runs along the Mekong River offers stupendous natural scenery. At the Pha Taem National Park, near Khong Chiam in the district of Ubon Ratchathani, an idea of the region's prehistory can be grasped from the rock eroded by time, where thousands of years ago, man painted his world of animals, hunting, and esoteric symbols. A narrow path, above the sheer drop to the river, follows along the mountainside covered by a think mantle of ancient trees, from where the rice paddies on the riverbank sparkle like emeralds. At the top, the curtain of trees opens in a clearing as the visitor's gaze ranges over the open green space. On the terrain of lava, smoothed over thousands of years, the petrified prints of possibly extinct animals and fantastic rock formations tell the story of years of laborious mutation.

The Mekong River with its murky waters, which become two colors, red and blue, in the sun, is the border between the Thai countryside and the mountains of Laos. In this land, men meet as they always have to bring the precious textiles from Laos that are embellished with designs and colors enhanced by women's imagination, the iridescent red lacquered objects from Vietnam, mechanical toys and imitation motorcycles from China, and imaginative products made from straw in Cambodia. The cities are peaceful but lively and full of activity with their low houses, gardens, and colorful temples. The most important and oldest monastery is Wat Phra That Phanom, near the city of Nakhon Phanom, with its galleries decorated with curious modern paintings and its bulb-shaped *chedi* in the style of the northeast, white with golden designs. In the villages, the temple with its annexed monastery is a meeting place for the community. During the day, when the adults are working the fields and the children are at school, the elders get together to enjoy the last stage of life, performing small tasks helpful to the others.

To the east, the Mekong runs quietly: here it is no long a border dangerous to cross but a means of communication between peoples and towns. The Kwai Noi River, which crosses the Sai Yok Yai National Park in the section of the tropical jungle near Kanchanaburi, is sadly famous for the Burma-Siam railway bridge, built during World War II by Allied prisoners. The park is reached through Nakhon Pathom, the place of origin of Buddhism in Thailand, where King Mongkut had a grandiose bell-shaped *chedi* built in the Ayutthaya style.

92 bottom left At Nakhon Pathom, the cradle of Buddhism in Thailand, King Mongkut had the Phra Pathom Chedi built. Building materials came from the ruins of the second sanctuary. The first had been destroyed in the 11th century by either the king of Pagan or by the Khmer of Suryavarman I.

92 bottom right In the Sai Yok Yai National Park, northwest of Bangkok, the Kwai River features lovely fluvial landscapes and an ancient jungle. One of its attractions is the very famous bridge and railway line, built in only one year between 1942 and 1943 by prisoners during the Japanese occupation.

94 top Even if you cannot speak Thai, it is not difficult to get your bearings among the luminous signs of the center of Pattaya. Restaurants, bars, boutiques, and nightclubs enliven nights in which no one ever sleeps. To recover one's energy, there is the beach in the daytime.

94-95 Even though there are now skyscrapers and the residential structures of the past have disappeared, Pattaya has not stopped to be a pleasant place for a brief stay. Along its two-and-a-half miles of beach, gardens, houses, ultramodern hotels, restaurants, and discos invite nothing but thoughts of leisure and entertainment.

The south features a prevalently marine landscape. East of Bangkok, the city of Chonburi is famous for its oysters, in Si Racha, on the beach in front of its red cliffs, delicious crabs are eaten in a spicy sauce, and the island of Si Chiang is a paradise for scuba divers. The most famous beach on the coast is Pattaya, a long bay onto which face luxury hotels, restaurants, and nightclubs, an extremely fun place to practice water sports and relax while shopping or visiting orchid gardens, Mini Siam, and the cultural villages with their elephant and Thai-dance shows. Furthermore, the nights are unforgettable. Peace and nature are nonetheless close at hand: in about a half-hour by boat, the islands of Ko Lan, Ko Phai, Ko Khram, Ko Samet can be reached, which have beaches straight out of a tropical dream and magnificent coral reefs with multicolored fish. Toward the Cambodian border, there are quieter beaches near Rayong and Trat, whereas Chantaburi is the city of precious stones: sapphires and rubies.

West of Bangkok, the Kra Peninsula extends in an endless series of white beaches and limestone cliffs as far as the Malaysian border. The panorama is captivatingly beautiful: the tropical vegetation of the rubber plantations barely recedes to make way for lakes, rivers, and waterfalls; the caves, adorned with stalactites, provide shelter to sea robins and bats in the darkness of their domes.

95 top The white skyscrapers of Pattaya overlook the foliage of the palm trees. Nonetheless, not even the capital of fun forgets that a moment of concentration is important for spiritual well-being. The temple, even though it has been recently built, maintains traditional Thai characteristics.

95 bottom The Thai Las Vegas is found in this colonial-style building. Here, the variety show is sparkling, lavish, and imaginative. Sequins, feathers, and spangles are the envy of Paris and its lido, with its gorgeous dancers, all of the male gender: it is the Tiffany's Show of Pattaya.

In the ancient cities of the south, once the theater for the battle to dominate the commercial sea routes, one breathes the peaceful air of the provinces. Petchaburi was chosen by King Mongkut to build his summer palace, the Khao Wang, located on a hill overlooking the city, and in the nearby caves of Kao Luang, myriad statues of Buddha and little *chedi*s pop up among the stalactites, inviting one to mediate within the silence of the earth. Nakhon Si Thammarat, whose historical Malaysian name was Ligor, was the capital of the kingdom of Tambralinga, which was forced to surrender to the emergent might of Sri Vijaya in the 8th century. Unfortunately, no trace has been preserved of the ancient realm, not even its main temple. Wat Mahathat underwent a radical transformation in the 13th century. Examples of the art of Sri Vijaya, the powerful maritime kingdom that stretched from Sumatra to the Malay Peninsula, are conserved at Hat Yai in the Museum of Southern Thailand. Crocodiles are part of the local wildlife, and it is possible to observe them, sleepy and not at all aggressive, at the local zoo. Songkhla features the spectacle of the boats painted in bright colors that are docked in its port. Hua Hin is the most traditional seaside resort town, still frequented today by Bangkok's upper crust, and where Rama VII had his summer palace, Klai Kang Won, built in the 1920s. Its long golden beach is bordered on one side by the rocky spur that gave it its name and on the other by the harbor where a lively nighttime market is held.

98 top On the triangular-shaped pediments of Thai temples, among the floral motifs sculpted and lacquered in gold, the mythical bird Garuda, the mount of Vishnu, spreads its wings. The frieze in the illustration is found in Wat Putha Nimit in the city of Phuket.

98 bottom In the city of Phuket are found houses of prayer of all faiths: mosques, Catholic churches, and Sikh, Buddhist, and Chinese temples. In the temple of Jui Tui, a lion watches over the entrance doors, holding its pearl ball in one paw and some coins symbolizing prosperity in the other.

98-99 The bay of Nai Harn, one of the most famous on Phuket, was hit hard by the tsunami of 2004, but within a few months it was up and running again.

99 top right On the west coast of Phuket, looking onto the Andaman Sea, a series of promontories form gorgeous bays with crescent-shaped beaches. Karon Beach is famous for its soft golden sand and the casuarina trees that frame it.

The most spectacular beaches and panoramic views of the sea are found to the west, along the coast and islands of the Andaman Sea, which took a full hit from the tsunami of 2004, an event that, thanks to help from the government and the shrewd management of international aid organizations, has left behind little more than a terrible memory. Patong is the busiest and most entertaining in terms of nightlife. At Nai Yang, in the national park of the same name, giant sea turtles deposit their eggs. Karon is the longest, whereas the most evocative, especially at sunset, is Kata, linked to the stupendous Nai Harn by a panoramic road. From Rawai, where the "gypsies of the sea" – sailors and pirates that used to travel the maritime routes around the Indonesian Archipelago – live, the boats of fishermen depart for the nearby islands.

98 center and 99 top left Everything is new in Patong Beach, where the tsunami wreaked terrible damage. In the terrible days following the catastrophe, the Thai people fully demonstrated their best qualities: loyalty, alacrity, honesty, and faith in themselves.

100-101 Declared a national park by the Thai government, the coastal Andaman Sea and the islands that dot its surface boast a vast variety of underwater and earthbound fauna and flora. Diving

in these waters, easy to reach from Phuket and considered among the most beautiful in the Asian seas, is considered by expert scuba divers to be an unforgettable experience.
Though the islands

are covered by impenetrable forests and their interiors are all but impassable, the wide sandy beaches and coral-lined sea floor are all explorable, and it is not uncommon to spot dolphins and whales,

including sperm whales. Custodians of this unspoiled habitat, the sea gypsies populate a pair of tiny villages on the islands of Adang and Lipe, living in total symbiosis with the sea and nature.

Small, gorgeous, and almost deserted, the islands are like dreams that rise from the emerald waters for the pleasure of scuba-diving enthusiasts. Here, the sea is beauty in its purest form: sheer cliffs seem to make landing impossible, as if to make the appearance of inlets of fine white sand an even more spectacular vision. In Viking Cave, with its entrance at sea level, ancient paintings of ships attest to the passage of sailors from many years ago.

To the north, Phuket is connected to the peninsula by the Sarasin Bridge and forms an enormous bay along the mainland coast. The waters of its sea make Phang Nga Bay look like a mirror from which stick out limestone stacks and little greenery-covered islands. To the giant rock of Ko Pannyi clings a Muslim village on stilts. Caves and arches patiently carved by millennia of erosion are covered with fairy-tale tropical vegetation; vines and roots hang from their vaults, and mangrove thickets can be navigated. A stalactite coiled like a *naga* gives the name to Tham Nak, whereas the entrance to the cave of Ko Ping Gan is guarded by an enormous cone of rock – perhaps it really is the secret hiding place of the "Man with the Golden Gun."

Beyond Phang Nga, in Ao Luk Bay, the Than Bokkharani National Park is found. Paths penetrate the vegetation, and in the silence broken only by gushing of the waterfalls and streams, at the base of the mountain, an underground river appears from between the slabs of rock.

The Tarutao Marine Park in the southern province of Satun is made up of three groups of islands, covering an area of 575 square miles, 80 percent of which is ocean. It hosts a wide variety of plants, mammals, birds, and butterflies. On the island of Ko Tarutao – the biggest – sea turtles come to deposit their eggs. Ko Adang, Ko Rawi, and Ko Batong with their atolls are surrounded by the most beautiful coral reefs in the Andaman Sea. Around their beaches, birds, fish, and other animals have lived for thousands of years in a primordial environment that knows no intrusions.

102 top Settled against the enormous stack of Ko Pannyi, in the Phang Nga Bay, the village of the "sea gypsies," the Muslim fishermen who originally inhabited these islands, is composed of houses on stilts, which make convenient docks for boats, and a green-domed mosque.

102 center At Bo Phut, on the island of Samui, the sea stays warm all year, the beach, though a bit rugged, has a particular kind of sand, and the bungalows offer good hospitality. A large golden statue of Buddha keeps watch over the quiet atmosphere of the bay and visitors' ability to relax.

102 bottom Along the coast of Phuket, the sea has a unique beauty: sheer rocks, fine white sand, calcareous stacks, and greenery-covered islands that pop out of the crystal-blue water.

102-103 *Paradise on earth, too fragile to last: that is how Ton Sai Beach, on Koh Phi Phi, looked before the tsunami of 2004. In Thailand, this was the island that suffered the worst damage, to the extent that they temporarily declared it closed to all visitors.*

103 *Penetrating the mangrove jungles and exploring around the monoliths rising from the sea of Phang Nga Bay, magic spots can be discovered in which fantasy can become reality without much effort. At Ko Ping Gan, one may encounter James Bond and the Man with the Golden Gun.*

104-105 *Francis Light was sent to Phuket in 1770 by the British government to establish a trading base under the crown's control. However, it is said that, having fallen in love with a pretty Thai girl, he abandoned the idea in order to marry her. The British crown had to be satisfied with the nearby island of Penang. Perhaps it is thanks to Light that so many beaches on Phuket, like this one, have remained unspoiled.*

*B*uddhism is a constant presence in the daily life of the Thai people. Here, Theravada Buddhism is practiced by those who believe that man's ideal state is achieved though the elimination of all desires and a total detachment from the world, with its texts in the Pali language because they came from Ceylon. Each day, rice, food, and flowers are donated to the monks, and much is contributed for the maintenance and embellishment of the monastery, just as sacred images are never lacking in houses, cars, and shops. The image of the Thai Buddha is lean, thin, with elegant and simple lines, in gold-layered metal or bronze, with half-closed elongated eyes, distinct eyelashes, an affected serene smile, and ears with elongated lobes. His head is covered with curls with a bun in the middle that rises into a flame, a gem-adorned crown, or a fan of protective serpents. Generally, the statues are in a seated or upright position, but in the Sukhothai style, a variant is found portraying the Buddha walking.

The Buddhist religion is based on the institution of monasticism. Whoever wishes to withdraw from the world and meditate becomes a monk: a person can even do this for brief periods, in thanks for kindness received, at the end of their university studies, or before beginning their life's work. Monks live on charity, wear a saffron-colored robe, and keep their head shaved and their feet bare. Everyone in Thailand respects the monks for their wisdom and good deeds: they practice therapeutic massage, help the poor, and give shelter to stray cats and dogs.

106 bottom left On a hill near Lampang stands the ancient temple of Wat Phra That Lampang Luang, one of the rare examples of a fortress-refuge. The warm tones of copper and gold of the chedi are repeated in the features of the statues of Buddha.

106 right The Golden Buddha in Wat Ko Keo Sutharam in Petchaburi has long-lobed ears, a sign of princely dignity, smooth arms rounded like an elephant's trunk, and lotus-bud-shaped hands.

107 Thai architecture bears Indian and Malayan influences. In Phra Boroma That in Chana, many small stupas recalling the opulence of southern Indian temples and the grandeur of Javanese monuments overlap in the form of the chedi.

The Thai temple is a symbolic representation of the cosmic universe. It has external walls that enclose the monks' dormitory, offices, a school, and a cremation pavilion. The internal walls delimit the sacred area and are decorated with beautiful frescoes or statues of Buddha, with doors guarded by the four mythical guardians, the warriors of the four cardinal points. In the internal courtyard the *chedi*, the *phrang*, and the various pavilions – on consecrated ground marked at the cardinal points by eight boundary stones called *sema* – are architectural expressions of the ancient cosmological concepts dictated by the sacred Hindu and Buddhist scriptures. In the middle of the universe as conceived by Hindus and Buddhists rises Mount Meru, the axis of the universe, symbolically represented by the *chedi* (stupa), and which governs the cycle of day and night, of the seasons, and therefore the harmony and well-being of man. Mythological characters and protectors, in other words, the statues, populate the cosmic universe. The guardian demons, the *yaksha*, guard the entrance, the *naga* serpents guard the waters of the earth and its underground riches, and the staircases are symbols of the rainbow and collaborators in creation. At the cardinal points, Garuda surveys the scene from the pediments on the pavilions, while at the top of the roof of the main *viham* or *phrang*, Indra, riding Erawan the three-headed elephant, reigns supreme over the 33 gods in heaven. In the forests of Meru – in other words the courtyard – mythical animals rove: *singh* the lion, *nora singh*, half man and half feline, and *kinnaree*, men and woman with the feet and wings of birds.

108-109 Young Thais, at the end of school and before getting married, retire for a period to a monastery to serve their novitiate. Every morning, they leave the temple's enclosure to collect donations. They receive offerings of food from the faithful, which contribute to their upkeep thus helping them acquire merit.

109 Perambulation, which must be done in a clockwise direction, allows monks of Wat Mahathat in Nakhon Sri Thammarat to perceive the importance of the stupa as a cosmic monument, a meditation aid, and a concrete symbol of the doctrine of the Dharma.

110 and 111 top
Under the engrossed gaze of the Bodhisattvas, the monk asks to be granted wisdom. The statues sit in the yoga position of meditation, with their hands in their laps and their palms turned up. The Buddha in meditation is attributed to people born on Thursday and protects teachers and magistrates.

Meru is the dwelling of the gods and guardians and is surrounded by four circles of continents and seven mountain chains, separated from each other by seas. On its far side stretches the great cosmic ocean in which are found the four major continents, which face the cardinal points, and finally the last mountain chain in which concludes the universe. Although the *chedi*, which contains the reliquaries of Buddha, is a symbolic figure, the *phrang* represents Mount Meru better architecturally because its sculptures symbolize the gods and the smaller *phrang* the lesser peaks of the mountain. Its galleries represent the mountain chains, whereas water in whatever form is the cosmic ocean from which emerge the four continents. The shape of the *chedi* and *phrang* also represents the three worlds of Buddhist cosmology, the three spheres of the progressive path to liberation, which include the 31 realms of existence, beyond which lies Nirvana.

111 center Monks are respected for their wisdom and the good deeds they do on behalf of the community. Among these actions, they practice therapeutic massage and help the sick and the poor.

111 bottom left Thai Buddhas have broad shoulders, narrow hips, and flat abdomens. The statues at Wat Haripunchai in Lamphun sit in the yoga position called pang man wichai on lotus thrones, symbols of spiritual elevation.

111 bottom right The monastic code requires that monks (seen here at Petchaburi) eat their only meal of the day before noon. They are allowed only vegetarian foods and are prohibited from consuming alcohol and drugs.

112-113 The traditional Thai house is composed of pavilions in which live the various parts of the family. This wooden house in Chiang Mai features the typical roofs of the north, crowned with offshoots sculpted in the shape of naga *serpents, called* kaloe, *to protect the house from evil spirits.*

113 top left The inside of the house contains open, empty spaces, while the ample windows let light in but not heat. The simplicity of this house in San Kamphaeng is made pretty and pleasant by the designs on the balusters, in the floor, and on the teak-wood ceiling beams.

113 top right That which may seem decorative designs are actually ingenious architectural solutions. The walls, beams, and pylons have no nails, and this house in Muang Boran, built using a fixed-joint method, can be easily dismantled and moved. The raised threshold of the doors prevents animals from entering.

112 top The phra phum, *the spirit of the earth, lives in a little temple in a courtyard near the entrance, in the spot determined by an astrologist. Inside the little house of the spirits, his image is placed, and if he so desires, it is necessary to give him a plaster horse, elephant, and maybe even a television or Mercedes as a gift.*

112 bottom Phii ruan are the spirits of the house, usually deceased family members to whom a house to live in must be assigned. They also need to be provided with fresh flowers, candles, and a bit of rice to eat. In turn, they watch over the well-being of the family and offer special help during difficult times.

The traditional design of Thai houses, born in central Thailand, was made perfect over thousands of years of experience and according to the demands of man and the territory. In wood, built on a platform on stilts, with a sloping roof that forms a triangular pediment on the front and covered porches on the sides, it has walls decorated with an elegant play of beams that, like the doors and windows, are prefabricated panels, united by fixed joints, and easily dismantled. The structure can withstand monsoons, is easily moved, is ventilated through spaces in the floor and wall panels, and has narrow, long windows to keep the inside cool and dry. The furnishings are simple: families live on the floor, of lovely, shiny teak with a warm color, and strictly shoeless. They sit on the ground, without tables, with a bed on a raised platform. A small altar for a statue of Buddha and a fireplace are never lacking. The houses can be single-family, but very often several houses are built on the same stilted platform for the children when they marry. On the porches, big jars in either glazed or unfinished terracotta conserve fresh drinking water. Along the rivers or canals, the entrance faces the water and a stairway doubles as a dock for boats or as a diving board for the children. The houses of the north have a roof that ends in a "V" called *kalae*, which complete the apex of the pediment. Sometimes they may seem like the wings of a bird in flight, but they more likely represent the horns of the buffalo and, since they are found only on the houses of the upper class, they are believed to demonstrate the family's prosperity. Above the door of the master of the house's bedroom sits a lintel called *ham yon*, meaning "magic testicles," as the room is the symbol of the family nucleus. Its size corresponds to the size of the owner's foot, and before engraving it with floral designs, either geometric or rounded, it is necessary to carry out a ceremony to invite the spirit of the place to enter the lintel and thus assure the couple's fertility. The construction of the house is linked with numerous rituals, which are performed after having consulted astrologists and monks so that the house, the family, and the community can live in harmony with the earthly spirits. The Thai worship the spirits, invisible and benevolent entities of nature. At the entrance to every house, but even to skyscrapers, there is a little dwelling or miniature palace for them in which the guardian spirit is invited to stay through a special ceremony performed by monks. Every day, they are offered a bit of rice, a flower, or a little candle: a well-attended spirit will offer its protection to the house and its inhabitants.

The Thai are not the only ethnic group living in the country. Besides Mon and Khmer and mostly in the north, tribes of Chinese-Tibetan origin, like the Lisu, Akha, Karen, or Austro-Thai, such as the Meo and Yao, live. They were peoples who often came to Thailand because of conflicts in their own lands; some of them were unable to gain access to any kind of education due to the language barrier and were, therefore, highly dependent on the cultivation of opium poppies to survive. In the last 20 years, the Thai government has enacted a policy of integration for the mountain tribes, which has greatly improved their living conditions without destroying their socio-cultural traditions. They generally practice rotation farming, are largely Animist or Taoist, speak Chinese-Tibetan or Burmese-related languages, and are overall monogamous, except for the Hmong, who practice polygamy. Their traditional clothing is truly charming: black with kilts and vests embroidered in bright colors using a cross stitch, decorated with heavy silver jewelry, no shoes, but with legs protected by embroidered leggings, and with fanciful hairstyles, also adorned with silver studs and embroidery. They smoke a pipe – even the women – and the shaman is the authority figure of the community.

116 top left The Lisu, who cultivate rice, vegetables, and, in the past, opium poppies, prefer to live in inaccessible mountains spots for defense purposes. They are Taoists but are also devoted to the worship of their ancestors and nature spirits. Shamans act as the intermediary between the human and supernatural worlds.

116 top right The base unit of society on the plateaus of Mae Hong Son is the village, consisting of families of the same ethnicity. Isolation, necessary in order to be near their cultivated lands, makes it hard to take advantage of health and education services, which are provided by itinerant personnel.

116-117 A succession of rings are placed around the necks of female Padaung children from when they turn five years old until their wedding day to elongate the neck like that of a dragon, from which they supposedly originated. The neck is massaged beforehand with an ointment made from dog fat, coconut milk, and the royal jelly of bees.

117 top Generally, Thai women do not smoke, at least not in public, but of course in rural areas they still practice habits that have disappeared from more populous areas. Tobacco is grown locally and smoked wrapped in specifically selected and dried leaves. In recent years, the government has launched several educational campaigns about harmful habits, from drugs to cigarettes.

117 bottom The denomination "hill tribes" indicates the ethnic minorities that live for the most part in the north, often originally from bordering states. Thanks to a 1976 decree, the government granted these peoples Thai citizenship, with the right to maintain their respective cultures and freedom of religion.

From the north comes the animal elected symbol of Thailand: the Thai elephant is medium sized, with small ears and a playful temperament, and is great help in transporting teak trunks, in the forests, and once upon a time, in battle. Still today, they are highly respected and loved, also because three-headed Erawan, the mount of the god Indra, was their brother. Each year in Surin, the "elephant parade" is celebrated, during which the most beautiful exemplars march around dressed in their finest, perform exercises of skill, and are used to play polo. Unfortunately, the times have changed and their work is now done by heavy machinery; for the elephants, it is time to retire. Funds are re-served to purchase unemployed elephants, but when they are brought to Bangkok to be entrusted to the care of the government, they can be seen walking among the cars, through the traffic jams. It seems rather a sad end, but these likeable animals have a thousand resources, and a certain number have already found a new job in the tourism industry. What is better than a visit around the ruins of Ayutthaya comfortably seated on the palanquin of an elephant guide? The great *chedi* can be seen better and it is fun to sway down the street, while the elephant greets drivers with delicate taps of their trunk on their windows. Careful though, tips are expected in bananas!

119 top right Wearing the traditional silk dresses, girls follow the historical elephant parade of Surin, a quiet farming town that each year comes alive with the arrival of tourists come to attend the folkloristic events, who return to the city after having purchased the exquisite, freshly-picked products of the land.

120 top left In April, the festival of Songkran marks the traditional New Year. It is the water festival, which transforms into a giant battle. In Chiang Mai, the holiday is particularly noisy, as water is thrown at passers-by and the streets become a fountain, however the shower is refreshing and invigorating.

120 top right
*Celebrated also in
Burma and Laos, where
it holds particular
importance in Luang
Prabang, the Songkran
Festival is not just an
opportunity to enjoy
oneself but also to
purify the body and
soul. Therefore, good
deeds must be
performed that will be
held in consideration
in a future life.*

It seems appropriate to conclude with holidays. The traditional holidays are numerous: Songkran is the Thai New Year, on April 13, and according to an ancient rite, participants launch sprays of water, a symbol of the rain showers that fall from the sky and, like sperm, fertilize the uterus of the world so that the harvest may be abundant. Likewise, in the northeast in May, enormous handmade rockets explode in the air to evoke the rains of the monsoons. On the festival of the full moon in May, in honor of the Enlighten-ment of Buddha, the king distributes fans to the monks who have distinguished themselves for their piety during the year. However, the most charming of all is Loy Kratong, the November holiday of lights: in honor of the mother of the waters, little boats fashioned from palm fronds are laden with flowers, a coin, and a small candle. The tiny vessels are placed in the water and float down the rivers of the whole country. The night is transformed into an enchanted world of little twinkling candles.

120-121 and 121 top
*Water, besides being
an instrument of
purification, is the
symbol of fertility,
the earth, and men.
On the first day of
Songkran, children
pour perfumed water
into the hands of their
parents. In Chiang
Mai, the water unites
the whole family in
an embrace.*

121 bottom
*On the first day of
the Songkran Festival,
images of Buddha are
splashed with water
and carried around
the city in processions,
in this case in Chiang
Mai. To gain merit
through a good deed,
fish to be freed along
waterways can be
bought at the market.*

122 In November, Loy Krathong fills the waters of Thailand with lights. In the charming setting of the archaeological area of Sukhothai, girls in traditional costumes gently place small rafts in the water in which they have put an offering of flowers and a candle to honor the goddess of the waters and rivers.

123 In addition to little candles, flowers, deftly prepared and placed on the little Loy Krathong rafts, are offered to the mother goddess of the waters and rivers. Incense sticks are inserted among the flowers; the night air is filled with lights and fragrances.

124-125 The krathong, *the floating devices offered to the mother goddess of the waters on the occasion of the Loy Krathong Festival, drift along the canals and rivers bearing their cargo of prayers. They are shaped like lotus flowers, but they also hold small golden* chedi *in honor of Buddha.*

INDEX

PHOTO CREDITS